Beyond The Secret

The key to the best seller and new revelations to improve your life

Brenda Barnaby

SHREE BOOK CENTRE

Beyond the Secret

ISBN : 978-81-8499-202-1

First Published: 2009

© Ediciones Robinbook

Originally published in Spanish by Ediciones Robinbook, S.L. Barcelona.

Published in India by
PENTAGON PRESS
Exclusively for
SHREE BOOK CENTRE
8, Kakad Industrial Estate,
S. Keer Marg, Off L.J. Road,
Matunga West, Mumbai-400016 (India)
Phones: 022-24377516, 24374559, 24380907
Fax: 022-24309183
Email: sales@shreebookcentre.com

All rights reserved. No part of this publication may be reproduced, stored in a retrieval system, or transmitted, in any form or by any means, electronic, mechanical, photocopying, recording, or otherwise, without first obtaining written permission of the copyright owner.

Printed and bound by Syndicate Binders, Noida.

Contents

Prologue 10

1. **The revival of ancient wisdom** 13
   An original thinking entity 16
   The creative power of the mind 17
   The power of mental vibrations 19
   A philosophy for success 22
   The importance of willpower 24
   The power is within you 28

2. **The opportunity of the new millennium** 31
   The great law of the universe 34
   The creed of the New Thought 38

3. **Learn to explore your mind** 47
   Analyze your current situation 49
   Practise deep breathing 52
   Breathing and Good Health 61
   Exercise your concentration 61
   Reject negative thoughts 70

    Overcome your fears 76
    Rehearse visualization 85

4. **How can you transform your life?** 97
    Achieve spiritual harmony and mental equilibrium 100
    Use of curative visualization 111
    Improve your love life 122
    Achieve your professional goals 135
    Achieve long-term financial well-being 146

5. **Spiritual and philosophical sources** 153
    Hinduism: the oldest religion 156
    Buddhism: the cult without God 159
    The Zen phenomenon 162
    Reiki: the energy that cures all 163
    Pythagoras and the Neo Platonic 165
    Franz Mesmer and animal magnetism 167
    The theory of emotional intelligence 170

Appendices
    Authors consulted while writing this book 173
    Centres of New Thought in Spain and Latin America 181

Beyond
The Secret

Confidently move towards your dreams,
in order to live the life you have imagined.
Henry David Thoreau

We know what we are but we do not know what we can be
William Shakespeare

We can become exactly what we want
Pico della Mirandolla

Prologue

The main reason to write this book was the firm assurance that we are living a unique opportunity. This assurance is manifested in the growing amount of mind-related movements happening in the first few years of this third millennium. The most concrete expression of these phenomena — the success of the audiovisual and printed versions of the book written by Rhonda Byrne titled *The Secret*.

The Secret was written in collaboration with more than twenty luminaries of metaphysics* and self-help movements. Byrne introduces us to a series of authors who explain the theoretical and practical elements of the Law of Attraction through mental vibrations. Byrne declares that this very old method was followed by several reputed personalities through history. Today, their "secret" is available to all, thanks to new guides and masters, like those who participate in this collective work.

We respect the professional work of Rhonda Byrne, as well as the clarity of her arguments while explaining difficult concepts. But most of all, we admire and share her enthusiastic faith in the secret power of our mind that is influenced by divinity in order to:

---

* metaphysics is understood as a philosophic theory not as an imaginary spectacle.

*Change our lives and obtain plentitude,
happiness; and the fulfillment of our goals.*

For that reason, this book is titled **Beyond the Secret**. We do not pretend to underestimate or try to prevail over the book by the Australian author, but to add to it as an important part of a much wider phenomenon. That is, to complement it with additional data, experiences, individual, secrets and advice that also form part of the "opportunity of the new millennium".

We believe that we could offer to the readers of this book a more complete perspective of this phenomenon, of the arguments that lead us to believe in the enormous energy of our mind. And, above all, we include a wide range of advice and exercises designed by the best amongst the current guides and masters.

I hope that in the following pages, you will find the motivation for and the path towards experiencing an extraordinary life.

Transform your life and fulfil your desires!

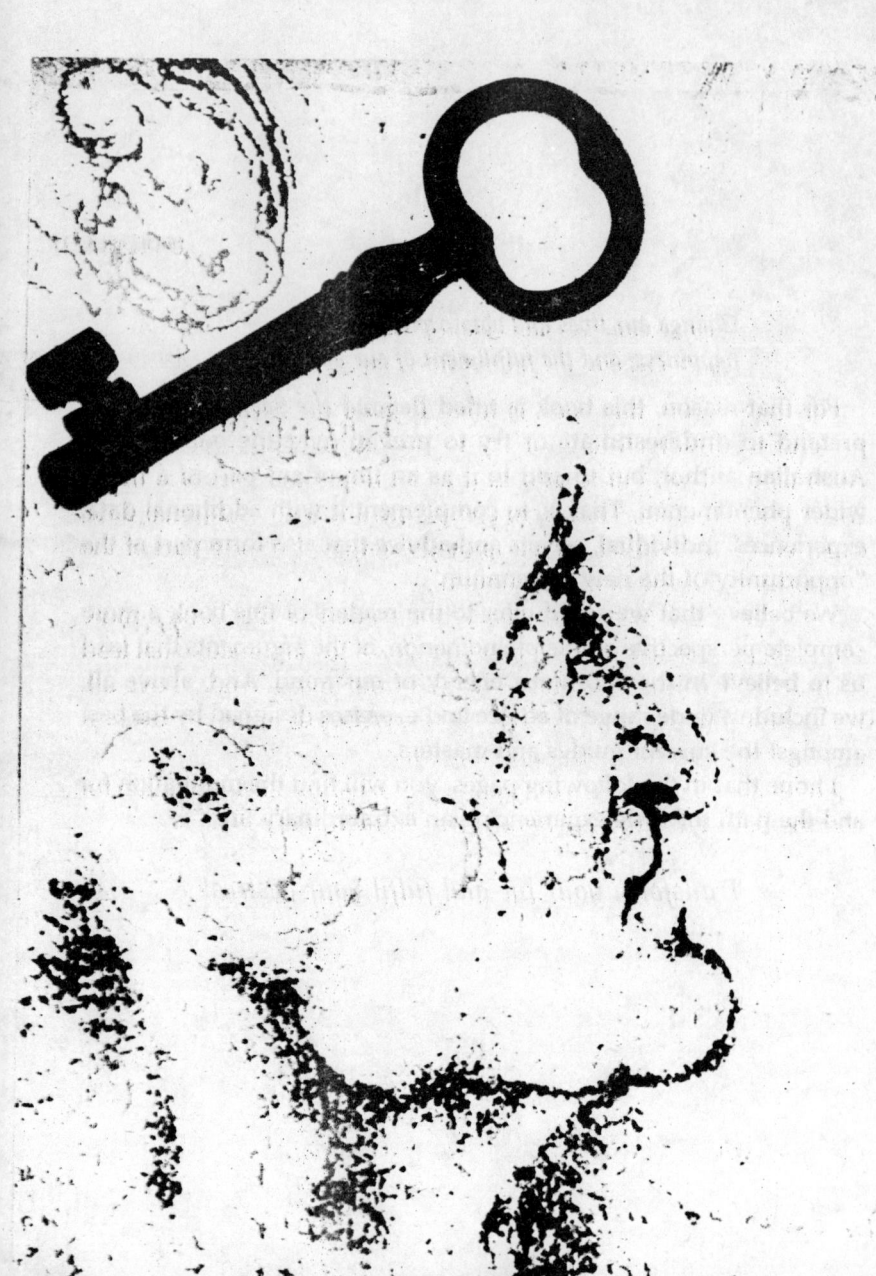

1.

The revival of Ancient Wisdom

*The universe is all about transformation.
Our life is like the thoughts that shape it.*
                                Marcus Aurelius

In olden times, knowledge was based on unity of the spirit, mind and body that, together, interact with divinity in creating and controlling the energy of the universe. The great ancient masters who zealously guarded this mysterious knowledge through the millenniums, allowed few individuals or selected groups to know of this knowledge. But their revelations were always partial, fragmentary and very often based on beliefs, ideas or tendencies of those who could experience them.

All the above made the transmission of wisdom doubtful and reserved till the end of the XIX century and the beginning of the XX when several important persons emerged with a more coherent and concrete vision that could overcome the tendency to prevent the spread of this magnificent legacy. Today, their search offers to all of us the opportunity to enrich our lives.

The resolution of the enigmas of this ancient wisdom was made possible by numerous intellectuals and researchers who studied and spread it by developing certain practices that now permit all of us to benefit from the virtues of this wisdom. As homage, we present a synthesis of the work of some of the most prominent scholars who help make the old doctrines more coherent.

An original thinking entity

WALLACE WATTLES (1860-1911)

Wallace Wattles is a very important figure as far as the revival of the knowledge of the ancient masters is concerned. Abettor of the so-called New Thought, to Wattles can go the credit that his book *The Science of Getting Rich*, published in 1910, inspired after almost a hundred years the research by Rhonda Byrne that enabled her to film and write her successful compendium *The Secret*.

> *The objective of our entire life is to develop ourselves, and all living beings have the inalienable right to the pursuit of such development as he or she is capable.*
>
> **Wallace Wattles**

Wattles' book depicts the concept of an original amorphous thinking entity from which emerged all that exists in the Universe. A kind of Borges' Aleph in which is concentrated all that exists as seen from all dimensions. In its initial state, this entity penetrated and filled up the "inter-spaces" of all cosmic planes. Therefore, Wattles explains:

> *A thought in this essential substance produces what this thought imagines. An individual can imagine things in his or her mind and if he or she prints this thought in the amorphous substance, he or she will be able to generate what the thought imagines.*

The idea of a creative relation between the mind and the cosmos comes from the ancient oriental *Dharmic* religions. Its principles were revived during medieval times using manifestations of alchemy, magic and thaumaturgy that were able to transform reality by creating or changing the intentions of spirit with the substance of matter. In more recent times, the theories of those methods and therapies mention the exchange of energy and vibrations between the individual and the Universe.

The principle proposed by Wattles to achieve a complete harmony with the amorphous entity, is to move from a competitive mind to a creative one. Otherwise, he assures, we cannot achieve harmony with the amorphous intelligence, which is the essence of the fundaments of creation, the creator of all of us. The real secret to getting in touch with the amorphous intelligence is by showing that we are grateful:

> *In order to be in complete harmony with the amorphous substance we must show a sincere and fervent gratitude for the blessings that it has thrown upon us. The gratitude unifies the mind of an individual with the intelligence of a substance and in this way the substance receives his or her thoughts. We can maintain ourselves on a creative plane only if we connect with the amorphous intelligence through a continuous and profound gratitude.*

The work of Wallace Wattles was immensely successful in the first half of the twentieth century and his philosophy influenced various philosophers and authors of great importance in the field of mind techniques and positive thought.

The creative power of the mind

JAMES ALLEN (1864-1912)

The English poet and intellectual, James Allen, published his book *As a Man Thinketh*, in the year 1902, which is considered a fundamental tool in spreading the power of thought. Allen experienced a kind of illumination when he was 38, and when he was working as an executive in a big company. He left his job and retired along with his wife to a modest hut in Devon, where he lived in a state of meditation and wrote numerous works on the importance of the energy of the mind.

A man literally is what he thinks;
his character is the sum of his thoughts.
James Allen

In this work Allen establishes an essential relation between our thoughts and our destiny; environmental circumstances and others' attitudes are less important, as it is our mind which creates those circumstances and those attitudes. This is how he explains it in a paragraph of his book:

Man is the master of his thoughts, the creator of his character who produces and moulds his condition, environment and destiny. As a creature of force, intelligence, love, and being the master of his own thoughts, he possesses the key to all situations and also has the potential to transform and change to make himself as he wants to.

James Allen's work reminds us that the human being has been created by divine law and is not an invention or an artifice. Cause and effect are absolute and inviolable in the virtual kingdom of the human mind as well as in the world of visible and material things. According to him, an accomplished and successful life is not obtained by a blind determination or by chance, but it is the result of constant and careful effort to find and enrich appropriate thoughts. He even says that the correct control of our thoughts leads us to divine perfection. And this is how he expresses it in his writings:

Man makes or breaks himself. In the artillery of his mind he has the arms to destroy himself and also the tools with which he can build the mansions of happiness, power and peace. By the correct use and selection of his thoughts he can rise up to divine perfection.

TO FALL INTO SELF DESTRUCTION OR TO ACHIEVE PERFECTION CLOSE TO THE DIVINE DEPENDS UPON OURSELVES.

The power of mental vibrations

WILLIAM WALKER ATKINSON (1862-1932)

Amongst the pioneers in this field stands out the name of William W. Atkinson, whose numerous books and articles helped in developing and consolidating the theory of mental vibrations. Lawyer, author and editor, he actively participated in the beginning of the movement called "New Thought", and ran a publishing house with the same name. For some critics his book *Thought Vibration or the Law of Attraction in the Thought World* published in the year 1906 is a reference work essential to the success of the publication of Rhonda Byrne´s book *The Secret*.

Every one owns a secret and latent individuality,
but only a few can express it.

William W. Atkinson

According to Atkinson's doctrine, we must understand this individuality as a potential force, as a superior quality of our mind. Most of us do not develop this latent individuality, due to lack of knowledge or just ignorance. The only way to activate it and to make it available to us is through a conscious control of our mental vibrations or waves. When a human being starts thinking about something, he unconsciously produces those vibrations, but generally those vibrations are dispersed and ultimately lost. But if we become conscious of these vibrations and concentrate to give them all the force available in our mind, they will achieve a considerable power and therefore they will reach wide duration and amplitude.

When an idea or a feeling is produced in a human being's mind, the force generated in the brain in the form of mental energy waves expands in the environment that surrounds this person up to a distance proportional to the energy generated. These mental waves are capable of activating similar vibrations in other peoples' minds that enter their field by following the laws of mental influence.

William W. Atkinson's theory of mental waves is supported by the advances of neurology and psychology that took place in his time, especially the experiments that proved that thoughts and emotions induce the elevation of temperature of certain zones of the brain. The heat stimulates liberation of energy, and all the energy is liberated through vibratory waves. If this occurs with light, electricity or radio, why not with mental energy? From this premise Atkinson offers this secret to make the best of our mental waves:

There is a lot of difference between the mental waves emitted unconsciously without knowing the laws of mental influence and those that are emitted with complete awareness of this phenomenon and directed by a powerful emissary. The force is the same, but the intensity of its force and its effects are determined by the conditions of the emissary.

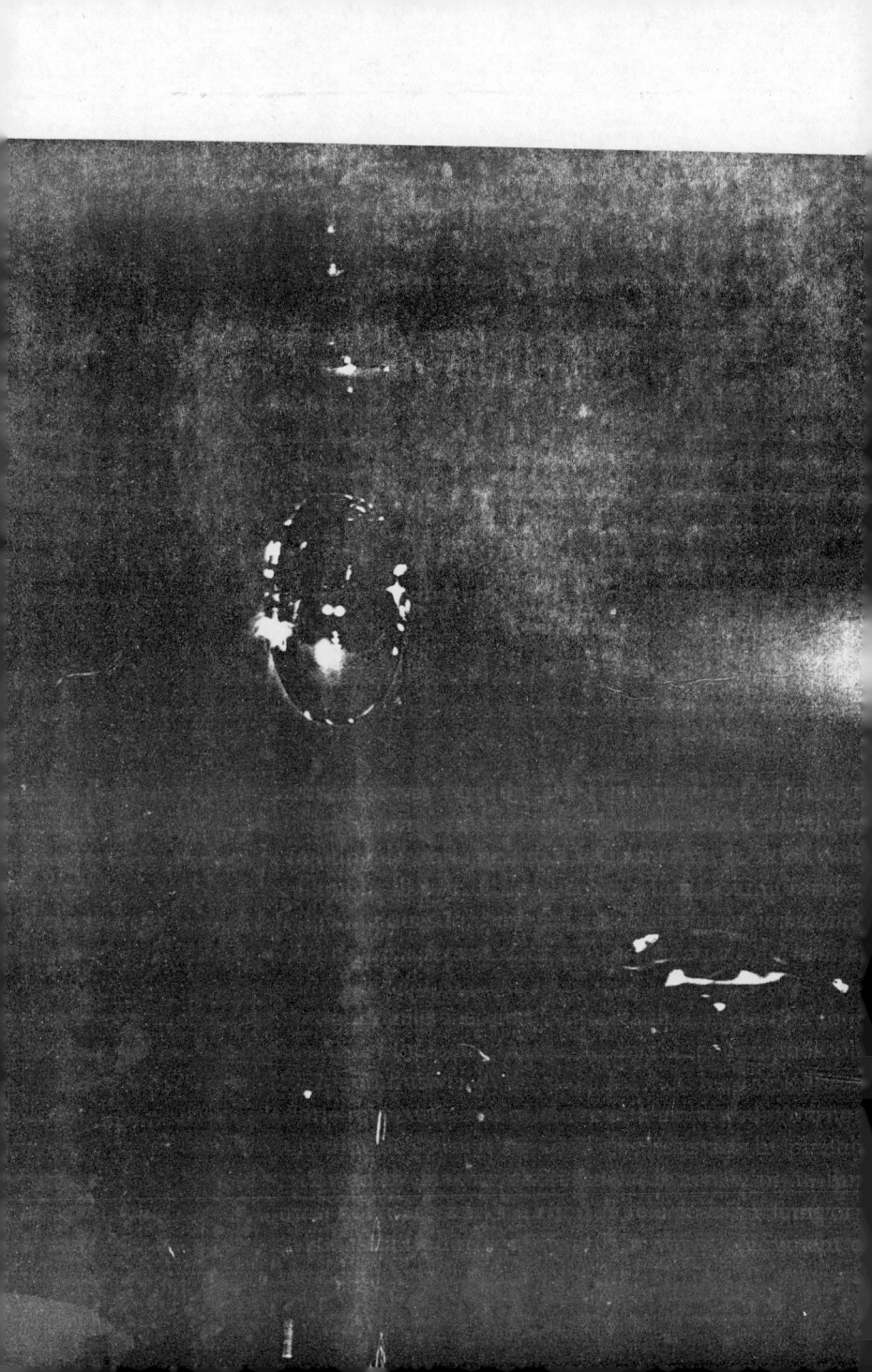

Atkinson practised his ideas and hypothesis on himself and that helped him to unfold an immense capacity for work. He published hundreds of books and articles in his name as well as in a pseudonym and he consolidated and enriched the New Thought movement. His passion drew him to a deep study of metaphysics and occultism. He was one of the pioneers of Hinduism and yoga in the West.

THE CONTROL OF MENTAL VIBRATIONS ALLOWS US TO INFLUENCE OUR ENVIRONMENT.

A philosophy for success

NAPOLEON HILL (1883-1970)

Professor Hill is the author of one of the most influential books of energetic mentalism and self help: *Think and Grow Rich*. He established the technique of adding to his theoretical ideas a series of practical advices for the reader that, later on, was followed in different ways by almost all writers that deal with the revival of the lost wisdom. He named his proposal *"philosophy of success"*, a term that, without any doubt, gives an insight to the personal, social and material character of his advice.

> *All that the mind can conceive and believe in, can be attained.*
>
> **Napoleon Hill**

Following Sigmund Freud's theory of psychoanalysis, which was innovative at that time, Professor Hill gave prime importance to the sexual energy, implying that the libido could be sublimated in order to better achieve objectives in other fields:

The sexual desire is the most powerful desire of human beings. Taken away from its push, individuals deeply develop their imagination, courage, will power, persistence and creativity in a much superior way than in normal circumstances.

For Hill, the desire to have sex is so powerful that in order to achieve it, one is ready to risk dignity, reputation or even life itself. But this potential energy can be channelized to other paths, maintaining its attributes. A soundly trained mind can divert sexual energy to achievements in social, artistic and professional fields. In his own words:

"The transmutation of sexual energy without any doubt requires a lot of will power, but the compensation is worth it. The desire for sexual activity is innate and natural. And it can neither be suppressed nor can it be eliminated. It must be given a form of expression that enriches the mind, body and spirit. If this transmutation is not achieved, this energy will wish to be spent through purely physical channels".

OUR MENTAL FORCE INCREASES WHEN THE SEXUAL ENERGY IS CHANNELIZED.

We must not think that Hill was some kind of puritan who condemned physical sexual practice. His proposal implies "taking on loan" a part of this energy or the whole of it, but never wasting it. His philosophy is based on control of the mind and follows Edison's principle on the cosmic relation between energy and matter which theorizes that the mind enriches itself from a physical base.

I know that the Universe is governed by an infinite intelligence; all that exists follow infinite laws.

Thomas Alva Edison

The importance of willpower

EARL NIGHTINGALE (1921-1989)

Author of numerous books on the topic of success, Earl Nightingale was an active follower of the ideas of Napoleon Hill, whom he quotes frequently as his master. His theory reaffirms the power of the mind, but he presents this mental force as deprived of cosmic or mystical connotations, instead centring it in the individual's capacity to dominate it. He is considered as the founder of the "motivational" movement within the field of self help, with a technique based upon willpower and concentration.

> *All you need is to know where you want to reach;*
> *the solutions will come up spontaneously.*
> **Earl Nightingale**

In some way Nightingale foresaw Rhonda Byrne as he received the illumination after having read the book *Think and Grow Rich*. Nightingale explained that he found the book of Wallace Wattles in the public library of Long Beach while looking for the answer to the following question: *how can a common man, without any special quality, starting from zero, achieve what is important for him, and in this way contribute with goodwill to others?*

Nightingale, inspired by the reading of Wattles, found the answer, or at least the path towards it. This discovery took place in the year 1957, and this very year she published her book *The Strangest Secret*, a title related to that of the Australian author (Byrne). According to Nightingale's vision the key to success starts by planning an objective followed by making efforts towards achieving it. But this objective must not necessarily be a remarkable position, fame or public success. It is basically directed inwards towards enjoyment of life at every moment:

To achieve happiness, we must not forget that we must never lack a goal which is important to us. To fix a purpose with deep personal interest; something we may enjoy doing for twelve to fifteen hours a day, leaving the rest of the time to think about it. What we impose and nourish in our subconscious mind with repetition and emotion shall become reality one day.

Nightingale thinks of the notion of success as a progressive achievement of a dignified purpose, whatever type it might be. We must propose some difficult and ambitious objectives in order to have an authentic personal challenge, but at the same time, it must be in line of our possibilities and the external circumstances that surround us. As soon as we fix an objective we are on the path to success because we are well aware of where we are heading to.

The author also insists on a positive vision of life that will serve to make conscious the fact that we have a personal objective. This gives us an enriched and generous vitality, a higher sensible perception of ourselves and of the world surrounding us.

Learn to enjoy every moment of your life. Be happy from now on. Do not expect any thing from outside of yourself to make yourself happy. Think about the value of your time available, at work as well as with family. You must enjoy and cherish every moment.

FIXING A DIGNIFIED OBJECTIVE HELPS US TO BE HAPPY AND ENJOY LIFE.

The power is within you

JOSEPH MURPHY (1898-1981)

Intellectual, author and personal guide towards development and growth, Joseph Murphy dedicated fifty years of his life predicating mental and spiritual power. He profoundly studied all the important religious doctrines and reached to this conclusion: "The power is within you!" With this inner conviction he presided over the Church of Divine Sciences in Los Angeles for three decades, wrote numerous books and delivered conferences and courses in various countries.

> *You shall be able to do marvellous things when you start using the magical powers of your subconscious mind.*
>
> **Joseph Murphy**

Murphy preached "scientific prayer". It consists of a harmonious interaction between the conscious and the subconscious levels of the mind in order to gain a particular objective. According to his philosophy, the control of this infinite internal power that lies within all of us will make us capable of attaining what we really desire from life. Faith is the main part of Murphy's preaching. It is not a mystical belief but the conviction that the inner power really exists and that one has to have faith in order to reach eternal happiness:

> *The law of life is the law of faith. And the faith can be summarized briefly like a thought in your mind. The way you think, feel and believe, shapes and conditions your mind, your body and your circumstances. To understand deeply what you are doing and why you are doing it will help you in reaching a subconscious realization of the good things of life.*

The technique proposed by Joseph Murphy aims to provide concrete solutions to concrete problems. Its objectives are oriented towards everyday conflicts that affect human life. These problems can be solved only by the individuals themselves using underlying forces that are still unknown to them. To learn and utilize these forces helps in confronting the problems and enhances the ability to solve them.

You desire a richer and happier life. Start using the power of your subconscious mind and you will see that your everyday problems smoothen out and you will attain harmony in your relationships.

Perhaps the secret of Murphy's great and continuous success lies in the relative modesty of his preaching. He promises neither fabulous riches nor ardent passions nor high profile triumphs, but a recipe to solve the personal and domestic problems that affect millions of common men and women in the whole world. He talks about personal harmony and healthy enjoyment of what is called "the good things of life": "All you have to do is to attach yourself mentally and emotionally to what you want and the creative forces of your subconscious mind will respond adequately. Start now, today, let the miracles happen in your life! And carry on till a new morning dawns in your life making the shadows disappear for ever".

THE SOLUTION TO PERSONAL PROBLEMS LIES IN THE FORCE OF OUR SUBCONSCIOUS MIND.

The intellectuals and authors introduced here and others similarly important like Ernest Holmes, Louise, Rober Collier, Emmet Fox or Genevieve Beherend, have been joining coherent ideas and experiences related to the functioning of the energy that lies in our mind. This knowledge and related proposals gave rise to the movement known as New Thought that, along with positive thought and the Law of Attraction, constitute what came to be named as "The Opportunity of the New Millennium".

2.

The opportunity of the new millennium

Man is mortal due to his fears and immortal due to his desires.
Pythagoras

Today is an opportune moment for us to improve our lives. The transition from the second to the third millennium has seen a change of an era, a cosmic transformation that influenced the coordinates of the Universe and its astral vibrations. With this phenomenon, substantial changes occurred in our understanding of the relationship between the underlying energy of our mind and the forces that interact with that inner energy to help us attain our objectives. Consequently, the present era is a propitious time for us to use the accumulated knowledge of intellectuals and spiritual guides to improve our lives.

Many of them already knew or had sensed the auspiciousness of our present and have already prepared the base for a renewal of efforts to tap subconscious energies. Their works have revealed the permanent union of the divine (of whatever name and shape) with our mind, our body and our spirit. That interaction is simple and smooth, as expressed with simplicity by a respected religious leader of extraordinary wisdom.

Neither temples nor complicated philosophies are needed.
Our own minds and our hearts are our temples.

Dalai Lama

Everything is prepared to enable us to **undergo a unique and transcendental experience**. The only thing to do is to sustain the desire to change our life, driving away fear, repression, **negative emotions and thoughts**. Now, we can enjoy the well-being and happiness that seemed impossible to us by using the latest **interpretations of the New Thought, the Law of Attraction**, positive **thinking and other mental and spiritual resources that** help us awaken **and use the potential of** our subconscious mind.

NOW IT IS POSSIBLE TO USE OUR HIDDEN ENERGY IN AN EASY AND EFFICIENT MANNER.

The great law of the universe

"As above, so below; as inside, so outside", **is one of the main laws** of the Universe revealed in ancient times by **the scholars and masters** of the mysterious great Hermes tradition. For them, this was the essential principle to attain perfection, **the power of magic and** occultism. The medieval alchemists recollected it and wrote it down in the Emerald Tablet or *Smaragdina Table*, **a cryptic text attributed to** Hermes Trimegisto, the Greek incarnation **of the Egyptian god Toth,** Lord of language and thaumatology.

The text of the Emerald Tablet

Without doubt, it is true that what is above us is also below us, and what is inside us is also outside us; this is the essence in which all miracles of the One are produced. As all things are created from the One, therefore, thanks to the law of transformation by thinking on the One all things come from Him. Its father is the Sun, its mother is the Moon, the Wind carried it in her tummy and the Earth is its nurse. The Father of all things of the world is here. His power is complete if it can return to the Earth. The One separates earth from fire, the subtle from the dense, and does so delicately, through His greatness and genius. The One goes up from the earth towards the sky and again comes down to the earth, and exercises control on the superior and inferior worlds. Thus, you can enjoy the glory of the totality of the world, and you will also be able to find your way in total darkness. This is the power of this powerful force because it is beyond the subtle and penetrates the physical body. The world has been created this way. From there emerge marvellous transformations. I am Hermes, three times as big, who has three parts of the world's philosophy. This is what I had to say about the Sun's creation.

In order to establish the Law of Attraction the great law of the Universe is combined with the Hindu principle, "one is all, and all is one". According to this law, all ideas, feelings or thoughts after synchronizing with their respective vibrations, attract their equals. In other words, if you think negative you will attract something negative; and if you think positive, you will attract something positive. One rule that arises from this idea is that one must not get obsessed with what one needs or what perturbs us, but must concentrate on what one desires to obtain.

The Vedas, ancient texts from India, contend that thoughts produce vibrations of different frequencies in the conscious mind. The reverberations of these vibrations are captured by minds that have the same frequency, triggering a chain reaction. The end result of this reaction is to attract spiritual or materialistic vibrations that have the same "wavelength" towards itself.

All is God

The first known explanation of the Law of Attraction dates back to the eighth century in the Kashmir region of India. Shaivism, a Hindu sect, based its philosophy on the existence of the *Spanda*, a Sanskrit sound meaning was already present in other Hindu sects, it was the vibration or resonance. Although this idea Shaivites who first described the concept in the well-known text called Spanda-Karika. In the next century, these texts were included in the sacred Vedic texts known as the Upanishads.

2. THE OPPORTUNITY OF THE NEW MILLENNIUM

*You are your deep and constant desire,
as is your desire, so is your will,
as your will, so is your effort
and as your effort, so is your destiny.*
Hindu Upanishad

The Upanishads remained unknown to the West for more than a millennium. It was only in the beginning of the nineteenth century that the French scholar, Anquetil Du Perron, translated the Upanishads into Latin. The translations evoked tremendous interest among scholars. As we have seen in the last chapter, a hundred years later, William Walker Atkinson published the *"Thought Vibration or the Law of Attraction"*, which became a Bible and a point of reference for various twentieth century mind study groups.

A hundred years later, the Australian Rhonda Byrne presented a compilation called *The Secret* where several experts expressed their opinions to spread the virtues of the Law of Attraction. This polyphonic, printed work was also produced in DVD format and has been received by a vast global audience that is part of the so-called new millennium movement. The law remains exactly as the Upanishads described it, and is considered eternal and immutable. What has changed is the understanding of its force and the resources to use it. These resources keep changing in accordance with developments in space and time. That is why, today we find ourselves in the middle of the expansion of the understanding produced by the transition of the millennium and we must take this opportunity to transform our life and achieve what we desire.

You are what you have been; you shall be what you do now.
Buddha

The creed of the New Thought

The movement named New Thought came into being from a series of religious and mystical ideas, summarized above, and based upon the spiritual vibrations of the mind. Most of it emerged in the United States at the end of the nineteenth century, from preachers who had been researching transcendental philosophy. The first person to use the term "New Thought" was Phineas Quimby, though figures like Ralph Waldo Emerson, Horatio Dresser, Mary Baker Eddy, Joseph Murphy and Ernest Holmes, can be considered pioneers too.

The soul is real and eternal; the body is unreal and temporary.

Mary Baker Eddy

We are warm and vital beings who think, feel, desire... I am in conformity with how we are and do not think that we should change. Great souls like Jesus, Emerson or Whitman who always offered us a deep understanding of spiritual wisdom, had simple loving and caring lives. They even had a good sense of humour.

Ernest Holmes

Ernest Holmes (1887-1970), a brilliant theologian and one of the most remarkable promoters of New Thought, was influenced by his family to join the Christian Science Church. There he became the disciple of Emma Curtis Hopkins. On the basis of Emma Curtis Hopkins' teachings and his own study of theology and spirituality, Holmes founded the Religious Science Church in which he preached a philosophy named "Science of the Mind". This was also the title of his book published in the year 1938.

Masters of the masters

Emma Curtis Hopkins was a brilliant female pioneer who postulated a new thought based on the principles of ancient wisdom. An iconoclast, a theologian and a women's rights activist, she abandoned the Christian Science Church to found her own movement in a theological centre at Chicago. Various generations of preachers took their training at this centre. Many of Hopkins' disciples founded new centres or churches within the framework of her ideas. For this reason, she is also known as the "master of the masters".

Ernest Holmes represents the most simple and, at the same time, the deepest spiritual version of the new thought movement. According to him, God is soul, and He is everywhere and in all things and beings of the universe. In human beings, the spirit of God is in our thoughts; it is His spirit that gives our thoughts its creative dimension. We must allow this dimension to grow and flow smoothly:

> We must think about ourselves as the way we want to be. We do not make the thought to be creative, but He. There never was a human thought; all thoughts are divine, thought within the human condition. We do not need to look for other powers, because we possess the greatest of all powers.

Of course, Holmes does not preach that we should wait for God to think for us. He exhorts us to recognize the divine nature of our thoughts and use them to fulfil our goals and our desire for perfection and fullness. In order to attain this, Holmes places a lot of importance on contemplation of life - with happiness and a sense of humour, without being beaten down by depression and hopelessness.

> *You must forget all negative arguments and*
> *think of those lesser but really positive ones.*
>
> Ernest Holmes

Followers of the New Thought generally are monotheists and believe in a single divine energy that created the Universe, which is in all parts and in all things, everywhere and within everything. They conceive all aspects of reality, material and spiritual, as unique because they belong to the universal energy. The main principle of their creed is that thought evolves and develops to create our experiences of the world. They put emphasis on meditation and concentration with the help of positive thoughts, on mental and spiritual self-esteem, on praying and showing gratitude through prayers.

The New Thought accepts a relation, small or big, with Christian doctrine according to the ideas of different churches and some of its disciples are even tolerant of followers professing other denominations.

Often, New Thought is frequently related with the *New Age* movement. However, the New Age movement is based on astrological concepts, something that New Thought does not approve of, and on spiritual romanticism in interpersonal relations.

WE CAN PROFESS TO NEW THOUGHT WITHOUT RENOUNCING OUR RELIGION.

New Thought is clearly very different from other major religions in terms of attitudes. Its faith is not immovable and dogmatic; on the contrary, the essence is open to the evolution of thought. It is not a static creed but an eternally developing mental and spiritual process. Its followers believe that as humanity gains more knowledge of the world, the church of New Thought must also evolve to assimilate new knowledge.

The five basic principles of the doctrine of New Thought applicable to all congregations are the following:

- God is the source and the creator of all. He is One, good and is present everywhere.
- We humans are spiritual beings, created according to God's image. The spirit of God is present in each one of us, and for this reason, each person is intrinsically good.
- We humans create our experiences of life through our thoughts.
- Positive thoughts are powerful because they strengthen our connection with God.
- It is not enough just to recognize these spiritual principles, we must also live and experience them.

Churches in the world

There are several New Thought cults around the world, mainly in the American continent, Europe and Asia. The most important of these is the Unity Church that has more than two million members globally. It was founded in 1889 in Kansas, its parishioners count up to 900 churches distributed in fifteen countries.

Five other cults have been recognized officially as the expression of the New Thought in the congresses organized from time to time. These are: the Church of the Divine Science, the Church of the Religious Science, and Universal Foundation for a better life, Huna and the Japanese Seicho-No-Le. This last one is spread along the whole Japanese archipelago and has reached other countries too through Japanese immigration, with a special presence in Brazil. Huna is a cult that was founded in Hawaii in the second part of the twentieth century. It propagates "the secret science that is behind miracles" and its followers combine some aspects of ancient Hawaiian magic with the doctrines of modern metaphysicists'.

When we find the right direction, all we have to do is continue walking.

Buddhist proverb

If we accept that the Law of Attraction is the prime instrument to achieve our desires and attain happiness, we know that its essential tool is thought. Our aim is to control our thoughts and direct them towards attaining our goals while simultaneously rejecting all obstructions that stand in our way. This is easier said than done. The question is: how can we control what occurs inside our mind?

What we understand by thoughts is not just the conscious reflection we do to analyze a subject or to take a decision. The mind also has ideas, feelings, fantasies, illusions, images and other spontaneous vibrations that apparently do not arise when we want them to. Can we avoid them or reject them when they do appear? And how can we guide our conscious thought in order to attain our goals?

The answers to these questions lie in the following pages...

The moment has arrived to start the journey that will totally change your destiny. Based on advice and practical steps it will enable you to reach the new existence that you deserve. If you follow them with faith and steadiness you will be able to learn how you can achieve your desires, hopes and ambitions by using the underlying energies of your mind to attract the powerful vibrations of the Universe.

DO NOT WAIT ANY MORE. START RIGHT NOW TO TRANSFORM YOUR LIFE.

We offer you a selection of concrete and simple advice from today's best spiritual leaders - masters and guides who have summarized all existing wisdom about the transforming power of positive thoughts and who are active in these first years of the third millennium.

TODAY, THE BEST SPIRITUAL AND MENTAL GUIDES ARE AVAILABLE TO YOU.

This selection is an open proposal - you can try and select those exercises that suit you the best. This will enable you to choose a method with independence and freedom - two basic qualities needed to live with fullness and harmony.

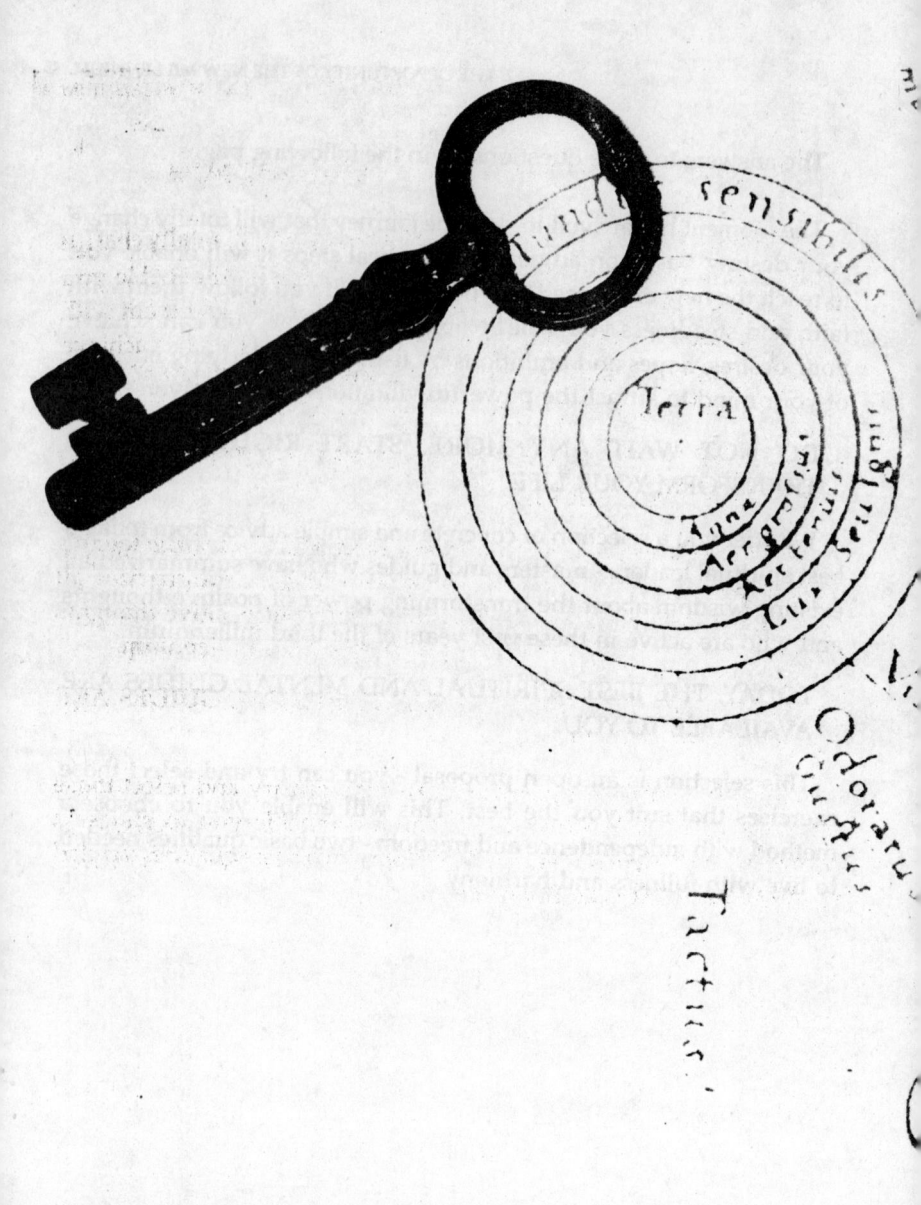

3.

Learn to explore your mind

Nobody can teach you more than what is already dormant within the light of your own knowledge.
Khalil Gibran

People use only ten per cent of their mental energy in an appropriate manner. The rest of it is lost in banal or negative thoughts or remains eternally asleep. These underlying unused energies represent an enormous potential waiting to produce positive vibrations that can attract the good things you expect from life.

You must accept that you do not know your mind and need to explore and identify it. This is the only way you will be able to dominate your mind and make it do surprising and marvellous things; in other words, make things you desire happen that you yourself prevented from happening. As a great Persian poet said: "You were born with a superior knowledge which is dormant, and there is nothing other than this. But some one must help to awaken it". In the following lines we explain the process to awaken this extraordinary knowledge.

Analyze your current situation

Vera Peiffer, one of the most successful present-day authors on positive thought and mental energy, has outlined a preliminary programme of great value in improving and transforming your life through the force of your own thoughts. The programme will also help you determine what it is that you really want to change. Vera Peiffer says:

> You need something more than just simple theoretical knowledge to bring a positive change in your life. You need to put these theories into practice, which means that you will have to assume the responsibility for your own well-being and stop blaming others for all the negativities in your life.

After this caution, Peiffer changes her tone and talks about the wonderful possibilities that such change may bring to you:

> In the long term, accepting responsibility for your actions is itself a successful strategy, as it opens the doors to a series of absolutely new possibilities for you to succeed. And when I talk about success, I imply diverse areas of life like health, money, happiness and personal satisfaction.

> There is no limit to what one can achieve when sufficient mental effort is applied.
>
> **Vera Peiffer**

Now we present a preliminary programme, adapted to make it brief and concise, as recommended by Vera Peiffer. It is important to read it carefully first and then put it into practice.

Dr. Vera Peiffer's test to assess present situation

- You must assume responsibility for your actions and feelings. They are yours and you are the only one who can actually influence them. Do not expect the external world to change, because that will never happen.
- Assess your present situation, keeping in mind all aspects: health, finance, work, personal relations, self-esteem, etc. Which of these would you like to improve?
- Make a priority list of the things you would like to change. You must concentrate on one thing at a time to ensure that your mind does not wander.
- Consider the first of your points. What is it about? Try to ascertain your attitude to the situation - what are the external factors that come into play? You will notice that in a majority of cases, there is very little that you can do to modify external factors. Therefore, it is your attitude that must be targeted.
- Decide on a concrete and precise goal. For example, do not say "I would like to be lucky at work"; instead say, "I am going to show that I really deserve a promotion". Establish a realistic goal, for example, "I want to be the head of the section this year" is more appropriate than "I want to be the director general". It will be easier for you to reach the first goal; this is the first step to keep improving.
- Do your basic work with enthusiasm. Controlling your mind will make many things possible for you but it will not work magic unless you put in extra effort. Work on particular areas like taking

good care of your health and your image, working hard, managing your earnings properly, being affectionate towards those you love, etc. Be careful that your subconscious mind does not work against your desires and ambitions.

- Eliminate from your mind and vocabulary the phrase "I cannot", because you will only put limits on yourself. If you really want something, you will achieve it. Remember that "I can" is there only because you think "you can".
- Avoid negative statements. Never say "I am scared". Instead say "I am calm and relaxed". The first sentence reminds your subconscious about fear and suggests that you might have it. But the second statement fortifies your sense of security.
- Imagine reaching your goal. Frequently visualize the moment when your desire has been fulfilled. Convince yourself that you can actually make all you imagine happen. Fill your mind with images of your new triumphant personality and you will actually start enjoying it.
- Stop looking for excuses, start NOW.

Practise deep breathing

The essential virtue of breathing is that it acts like a transmitter between your body and mind. Oxygenation is not only necessary to remain alive but also to provide an excellent connection with the inner self. The energy generated by the process of breathing, when it reaches the dimension of internal consciousness, facilitates mental vibrations harmonious to our whole being at all levels.

According to the philosophy of yoga, one of the seven ancient philosophical and religious practices of Hinduism, there is a direct relation between breathing and the state of the mind. When an individual is anxious, anguished or scared, his or her breathing becomes fast, superficial and irregular without any extra physical effort. This means that when the mind is agitated, so is respiration. On the contrary, a serene and restful mind makes breathing more regular, slow and calm.

It is not difficult to understand that if the mind influences breathing, breathing, in turn, also influences the mind. Oriental religions recognized that breath control is the key to mind control that opens the gate to positive thoughts, good vibrations and the achievement of our desires.

THE FIRST STEP IS TO CHANGE THE INTENSITY AND THE RHYTHM OF THE WAY YOU BREATHE.

The naturalist and spiritual therapist, Peter Ragnar describes the complete process of deep breathing thus:

> *The stimulation of the first cranial nerve, when air enters the nasal passage at the base of the cerebrum where the olfactory nerves end, produces vivid mental images. Regular practice of deep breathing eliminates the factors that distort the understanding of our consciousness.*

Ragnar says that, through breathing, we attract information vibrations that are not captured by any of our other senses. He compares it with the antennae of insects and with the tail, hair or feathers of certain animals that react on receiving non-sensorial information. Where are the antennae in humans? This is how the writer explains his theory:

Let us suppose that the fine hair along the mucous membrane of the nose are tiny antennae that capture electromagnetic vibrations. We know that information travels by the emission and reception of waves from towers and satellites. Can we also capture information through a physical antenna and take it to our brain? Why would it not be true, given that animals, birds and insects do it constantly?

All information is vibration till the cerebrum processes it as an image inside our minds.

Peter Ragnar

These reflections lead us to the conclusion that deep breathing fulfils two essential functions when connected to our mind: first, it stimulates visualization or thoughts and their conscious control. Second, it provides us with extra-sensorial information that originates in the external world. And when we mention external world, we include vibrations that have a cosmic dimension.

DEEP BREATHING CONNECTS YOUR MIND WITH YOUR UNKNOWN AND MYSTERIOUS INNER SELF AND WITH THE COSMOS.

Let us now recall the advice of Doctor Vera Peiffer, the author of a very simple and practical method to exercise deep breathing. For beginners, it is a very convenient exercise as it combines relaxation with diaphragmatic breathing in a simple manner within a short period of time. This is how Peiffer describes the exercise in her book *Positive Thought*:

- Adopt a comfortable posture, be it sitting or lying.
- Do not cross either the arms or the legs because this provokes physical tension.
- Place one hand on the stomach just above the navel.
- Look for main points of tension and relax them consciously. Relax

your jaws but do not open the mouth. Let your shoulders fall. Open your hands and relax your fingers.
- Close your eyes and be conscious of your body's parts: first the head, then the arms, the trunk and then the legs.
- Breathe normally, listen to your breath, at least the first ten breaths.
- Start breathing deep, filling the belly first and then the lungs, in one inhalation. Make sure that the hand on the navel rises before the thorax,
- Retain the air and count up to five. Exhale.
- Repeat ten times
- Let your breathing normalize naturally.
- Tense muscles softly
- Open your eyes while you relax your muscles again.

Dennis Lewis is one of the major experts in deep breathing and he calls it authentic or natural breathing. He prefers this name because he has often noticed that when someone is asked to breathe deeply, he or she contracts the belly and shrugs the shoulders – exactly the opposite of what should be done. In his works, he insists that respiratory control is the key to self-recognition and to understand the physical basis of transcendental meditation:

> *Breathing simply means to fill our inner selves with the positive energies of life; literally it means to be inspired. To exhale is to vacate our selves, to open up to the unknown, to feel that something has ended and to initiate a new journey. By paying close attention to the changing rhythms of the primary breathing process we start to awaken our inner power, the power that leads us to plentitude.*

Deep breathing is fundamental to physical health and spiritual development.

Dennis Lewis

Lewis is a **devoted practitioner and promoter of the immense benefits of correct breathing.** His knowledge of Oriental philosophies has helped him understand that the mere act of breathing is a kind of miracle that occurs every day and offers infinite possibilities of attaining perfection. In his words:

> *For thousands of years, the control of our breathing has been an integral part of meditation, which means it is also an integral part to the discovery of our inner self. Through breathing, especially when it is serene and simple, we can draw our mind towards the deepest parts of the extraordinary temple that is our body.*

The exercise of natural breathing
(Dennis Lewis)

This breathing exercise is easy as well as efficient. If practised for fifteen minutes every day for a few weeks, you will notice its benefits in your body as well as your mind.

- Sit down on the floor or in a chair, with your back straight and the legs crossed, like the lotus flower. If you do not feel comfortable in this posture, simply place your feet on the ground with legs folded at right angles (at the knees). If you are on the floor, stretch your legs, slightly open. In any case make sure that your back is straight.
- Cross your hands on your lap or place them on your knees, palms facing downwards. Feel your body weight being supported by the

universe and be conscious of your body parts and their vital functions.
- Start following your respiration mentally while you inhale and exhale. Be conscious of its rhythm, which will help you breathe fully. Be aware of the temperature and vibration of the air as it progresses through the nasal passage towards the throat, the thorax, and finally the lungs. When you exhale, follow the same path in the opposite direction to return the air to the air. Do not manipulate or alter your respiration, let it flow naturally for at least five minutes.
- Without losing consciousness of the breathing process, rub your hands against each other to warm them and then place them on your navel to feel the interior of your tummy. Try to perceive the way the heat and the energy of your hands influence your breathing. When you inhale, your tummy expands; and when you exhale it tends to contract making it flat.
- As you become conscious of these respiratory movements, you start experiencing a concentration of energy, some three to six centimetres below your navel. When you inhale, you feel this energy filling the entire belly and the thorax. When you exhale, the energy is concentrated in the form of a more compact force.
- Enjoy the generation of this energy for a few minutes. When you decide to stop, just give yourself a couple of minutes to feel the absorption of at least a part of this energy in the cells of your belly and spinal chord. Then, visualize yourself as a breathing human being.
- At the end of the exercise you will feel your body relaxed and your mind more serene and open - just like an authentic "breathing entity".

WITH ONLY FIFTEEN MINUTES OF NATURAL BREATHING EVERY DAY YOU CAN FILL YOURSELF UP WITH NEW ENERGIES.

As we have seen, deep breathing is one of the fundamental aspects of yoga. Its aim is to integrate the individual with the infinite; and to attain it, yoga works on the body, the mind and the spirit to bring them together to achieve fulfillment. It is believed that the practice of yoga, based upon physical postures, techniques of meditation and breathing exercises started more than 5000 years ago.

Inhale, and God comes near you. Maintain the inhaled air and God will remain with you. Exhale, and you go near God. Maintain the exhaled air and you hand yourself up to the God.

Krishnamacharya

Hatha yoga is the most known form of Yoga in the West. Its breathing technique, the *pranayam*, defines three phases related with the three main body cavities: abdomen, ribs and clavicle.

Pranayam Yoga Method

These exercises can be best done in a comfortable and relaxed atmosphere, with eyes closed be it on the bed or on the floor. Once you have had enough experience of practising this, you will be able to do them in any place or situation.

1. *Abdominal Respiration*
- *Inspiration:* inhale slowly, directing the air towards the abdomen. You will notice the abdomen is filled up due to the air pressure on the diaphragm.
- *Initial exhalation:* exhale fully many times, in a slow and prolonged way, trying to expel all the air from your interior.

- *Profound exhalation:* After many repetitions, you will notice that you inhale more deeply and that the breathing centres in the abdomen; then when you exhale, pronounce the sound of the mantra "OM" loudly (first the vowel OOOO...., and then in the end, MMMM); this will help make exhalation slower and more continuous, as the thorax box and the abdominal zone relax.

2. **Rib cage respiration**
- *Preparation:* It is good to do this exercise seated and relaxed in order to be able to vacate the lungs properly and to contract the abdomen.
- *Inhalation:* Keep the abdomen contracted and inhale slowly; you will notice that the air fills your lungs and the ribs expand covering the rib cage zone; this exercise needs more effort than abdominal respiration requires.
- *Exhalation:* Let the air come out in a very slow and continuous manner; you will notice that first the rib cage zone is vacated and then the lungs; contract the diaphragm slowly in order to expel the rest of the air from the abdomen.

3. **Clavicular Respiration**
- *Preparation:* Sit in a relaxed posture. Contract the muscles of the abdomen and the thorax as much as you can, even putting pressure on them with your hands.
- *Inhalation:* Raise the collar bone with shoulders backwards; keep the pressure on the trunk and slowly inhale as much air as you can; you will see that it is not much but its location engenders a feeling of fullness during breathing.
- *Exhalation:* Let the air come out slowly, and then relax the muscular pressure on the trunk in order to expel the rest of the air from the abdomen.

4. **Complete Respiration**
It is a combination of the three exercises explained above; it aims to clean up and fortify your body and to stimulate your mental energy.

In this case, you must start with breathing out:
- *Deep breathing out:* vacate your lungs completely, pressurizing first the abdomen and then the chest.
- *Successive Inhalation:* slowly collect some air, relaxing the diaphragm in order to fill the abdomen; then expand the chest to fill up the costal area completely after which, raise your collar bone in order to inhale some more air if possible. Retain the air for a moment and exhale slowly.

COMPLETE AND DEEP BREATHING FACILITATES BODY-MIND RELATIONSHIP.

Breathing and Good Health

Good physical health is one of the direct benefits of deep breathing. The diaphragm is joined around the lower end of the thoracic box and has an elongation reaching the lumbar vertebra. The deep breathing movement makes the diaphragm come down and massage the liver, the stomach and other organs. Later, during exhalation, the diaphragm goes up to massage the heart.

At the same time, the up and down movements of the abdomen and thoracic box help massage and detoxify our internal organs and improve blood circulation and the peristaltic function. The movement also pushes lymphs more efficiently in the lymphatic system.

Deep breathing is the formula to reduce any type of tension.
Byron Nelson

Exercise your concentration

Concentration is an indispensable tool to help control mental energy. All scholars and masters of mind-related studies in its numerous forms have dedicated a considerable amount of time, thought and experience to this very important aspect of thought control to enable the Law of Attraction to act.

Proponents of positive thought as well as medical research in the fields of neurology and psychology have proved that most people normally employ very low levels of concentration. Thus, it is probable that your capacity to concentrate is more than you normally use. Therefore you must learn and practise techniques of deep concentration, as these will make you exercise your mental power. That "the concentration power of an individual gives us the dimension of his or her greatness" is axiomatic for metaphysicists.

TO LEARN TO CONCENTRATE IS THE FIRST INDISPENSABLE STEP TOWARDS CONTROLLING YOUR MIND.

"To concentrate is to focus directly our conscious mental faculties on a unique object, without any kind of distraction". This definition by the psychologist Waldo Vieira describes, in a very simple fashion, the process of concentration. It is obvious that "unique object" here is not only material things but also virtual objects, images, ideas or as we shall see later, visualization of our desires. He explains it in this way:

> *In fact, a person who wants to project his conscious mind does not need any thing else but a strong determination to achieve his or her desire. This determination makes the achievement of your desire inevitable, something which cannot be achieved solely by the intelligent actions of the conscious mind.*

It is possible that you might think that it will be very easy for you to concentrate on a mental image and to maintain this concentration firmly. You can even think that you have already done it many times; for example by visualizing the face of a person you love or a place that you want to visit. But these are partial and incomplete experiences when compared to the true power of mental concentration. Try maintaining it for five minutes, without any type of associated images, distractions or interruptions. You will see that, in fact, it is very difficult and it is unlikely that you will be able to do it.

This is so because our mind usually flits from one topic to another, thinking about various things at the same time. The mind's attention is constantly solicited by new attractions and very often it chooses arbitrarily. Many of those who claim to be good concentrators in fact let themselves be taken away by the thoughts that surround them and make them forget all other things, especially when they are performing some daily chore or are listening to an uninteresting conversation. This is not an example of mental concentration but of simple fantasizing. In other words, those who experience these fantasies actually dream awake, without putting any effort to concentrate and direct the mind's vibrations towards positive thoughts.

TO CONCENTRATE IS NOT TO DREAM AWAKE BUT TO FOCUS OUR THOUGHTS.

The fundamental element of concentration is the ability to pay attention, which in turn depends upon your willpower, or, in other words, on your dedication to exercise this faculty of your mind even in everyday life. Of course you use attention whenever you need it: while studying or reading important news, while watching a film or a detective series on television, while doing something difficult or practicing a complex hobby as well as in situations that do not permit any kind of carelessness such as crossing a street without traffic lights.

In these and similar cases, you pay attention spontaneously, almost without the interference of your conscious because your mind is prepared and trained by experience to react this way. Children, who have not yet got the experience and mental dexterity of adults, generally have a greater tendency to be distracted.. But this, let us say natural, attention is not sufficient to achieve deep concentration. Practitioners of mentalism in the West as well as in the East advise us that doing exercises to develop attention is a preliminary step to the full-fledged practice of concentration. Here are some examples:

Talent without deep attention does not mean anything.

Helvetius.

Make the best of your opportunity

A well-trained mentalist is capable of concentrating on a topic or an object with surprising intensity. He or she is completely absorbed in thought and unaware of other things. But once the goal or object of his concentration is fulfilled, he can take his mind off the matter, feeling perfectly fresh and ready to undertake other tasks.

It is unlikely to be any different in your case. If you think that practising concentration, attention and visualization can interfere with your daily activities, it is because of erroneous or incomplete training. On the contrary, if you do something as it should be done, the power of your mind and its positive vibrations would trigger off a transcendental improvement in all aspects of your life.

YOU CAN REHEARSE YOUR CONCENTRATION IN YOUR DAILY LIFE.

Although you can keep repeating some of the attention and concentration exercises as a preliminary rehearsal to a more systematic and regular practice of concentration, there will be a moment when you will feel ready to undertake this practice seriously. In any case, hurrying up is not recommended because apart from being a symptom of negative anxiousness, hurrying could result in mistakes that force you to start the whole process all over again. So it is strongly recommended that you move to serious practice only when you feel completely sure of yourself... although if you make a mistake, it would not be the end of the world.

Peter Kummer, a well-known expert on visualization, stresses the importance of practice without dramatizing possible initial failures. He explains it in the form of an interesting analogy:

> *Just as we swallow water while learning to swim, it is nothing but natural to commit some mistakes and errors while trying to learn the application of positive thought. But as it usually occurs, these small stumbles just contribute to the learning process and with time help improve the levels of our experience.*

Kummer's own successful experience has led him to the conclusion that it is worthwhile to invest time and effort to use our mind positively.

> *Laws and mechanisms for mental development do exist and they help us redirect our life towards good health, fortune, success, love, harmony and financial well-being. You can achieve all of these and make them last forever.*

Something can be learnt well only by practising it.
Peter Kummer

We have designed two preliminary programmes for you to be able to develop deep concentration. Both of them can be executed easily and have proven to be efficient. These programmes are amongst the most practised in centres of positive thought and deep meditation. You can choose one of them or practise both alternatively. We want you to have the freedom of choice to transform your life according to your personality and desire.

Let us now describe the first system, based on the visualization of numbers and objects.

Numeral method of developing concentration

- Sit in a relaxed position, close your eyes and concentrate on the number one. When you start seeing it clearly, quietly start pronouncing the word "one". Forget the number one and start concentrating on "two", later on pronouncing the word "two" quietly. Carry on with successive numbers till you master this exercise.
- Concentrate on a blank point on the wall; keep your mind blank, paying attention only to your breathing process. Keep counting each exhalation. Do it as long as you can.
- Close your eyes again. Rid your mind of all thoughts and repeat the previous exercise of counting exhalations, breathing with the diaphragm at a normal rhythm.
- Place a small object (a coin, a pencil, a candy, etc.) in front of you. Concentrate on it while relaxing each muscle of your body. Observe the colour, shape, volume, and consistency of the object in front of you without allowing your mind to be diverted from it. Then close your eyes and try visualizing the object, reproducing all the details that you have observed.

The most important aspect in all these exercises is to keep the mind clear. If at some point you feel that you are not concentrating, stop at once, take a break and start all over again.

DO NOT LET ANYTHING DISTRACT YOU WHILE YOU ARE EXERCISING.

In the last exercise, we recommended you concentrate on some small object. This exercise involves the use of a candle or, to be more exact, its flame. For the ancient mystics, the candle was a metaphor for a human being: the body of the candle representing the body, the wick the mind and the flame the spirit or the soul. This is where the symbolism associated with the candle comes from.

Gerina Dunwich, a modern-day witch and a scientist, describes it in the following words:

> *The flickering flame of a candle radiates a mystical power. For centuries, magicians and sorcerers have used the candle to make a perfect atmosphere for enchantments or for meditation and prediction while keeping evil influences at bay. The use of candles in magic rituals symbolizes the creation of light to ward off darkness.*

On the other hand, a shining light in the dark is an evergreen reference of the cosmic, a point of attraction for vision, a guide for nocturnal travellers. The candle plays this role of attracting and concentrating the best vibrations of our mind in mentalist techniques. In a way, it is as if its wavering, amber flame exercises a hypnotic power that starts the Law of the Attraction.

Concentration exercise with a candle

Waldo Vieira, already quoted by us, adopted and compiled some traditional techniques to prescribe the following exercise:

- **Preparation:** Dress in loose, light clothes, without any belts, elastic or other accessories that might make your body feel tied down. Look for an isolated, tranquil, silent room, and exercise at a time when nothing can disturb or interrupt your activity.
- **The master candle:** Place a medium sized, white candle in a corner of the room. Light it and switch all the lights off.
- **Relaxed position:** Sit down in a comfortable chair, some three metres away from the candle. Keep your back straight and place your hands on the thighs.
- **Concentration:** Look at the flame without letting yourself be distracted, follow its oscillations, observe its colour till you feel that nothing else exists in the whole world but this flame.
- **Repetition:** Repeat this exercise daily, or at least thrice a week, till you have mastered it.

During deep meditation, the flow of concentration is as continuous as the flow of oil.

Patanjali

Reject negative thoughts

Once you have mastered the exercises described above, you are ready to work on your thoughts, recognizing and analyzing them. Our goal is to get rid of negative thoughts and fears that could hinder the fundamental transformation that you want to undergo.

In fact, we keep thinking the whole day; mostly to pay attention to what we are doing, saying, listening to or reading. But there are also thoughts that come up spontaneously say, for example, when the mind wanders over a set of paintings, remembers past situations or

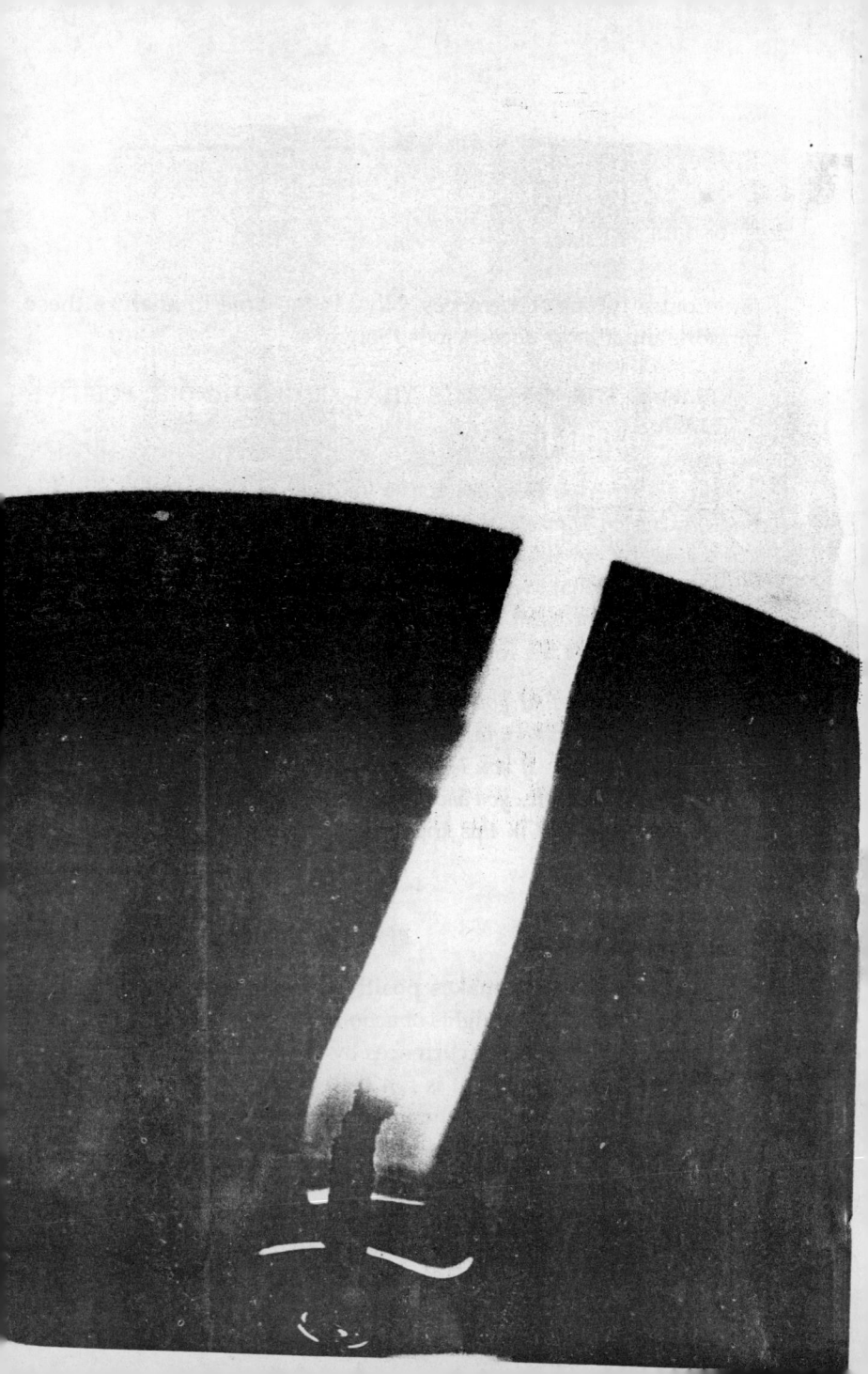

anticipates future occurrences. Now is the time to analyze these random and almost unconscious thoughts.

REMOVE THE THOUGHTS THAT COULD HINDER POSITIVE CHANGE.

Marty Varnadoe Dow, an active follower of James Allen and his book *As a Man Thinketh*, divides thought into three broad categories: knowledge of what I do and others do (that is thoughts of action); knowledge of what I wish (that is positive thoughts); and knowledge of what I do not want or hurts me (that is negative thoughts) She illustrates it using the following example:

Let us imagine that you are going to undergo a surgery. If you consider yourself lucky to be in the hands of a good surgeon, you are a positive thinker. If you learn every thing about the surgery, the process, the team, etc., you have thoughts of action. If you worry about what could go bad in this kind of surgery, you harbour negative thoughts.

Negativity not only makes positive thoughts difficult but also inhibits and paralyzes thoughts of action. Many people think that they can prevent unfortunate occurrences by thinking over them. In fact, what they must think about is not the eventual suffering that they might have to undergo but the ways to react so as not to suffer so much. For example, if you are driving up the hill beside a heavy vehicle, thinking that the truck will fall backwards and destroy your car would not help you in any way. It will be more useful to reflect over the ways to avoid such a situation or to reduce its consequences; you must, above all, have faith in your reflexes as a driver in this situation.

Thus, it is basically all about recognizing negative thoughts and getting rid of them in order to create space for the positive thoughts essential for the emission of the favourable mental vibrations that help you to achieve your desires and ambitions. Varnadoe Dow says:

You are not your thoughts, since they are just an activity of your mind. You have the right and the responsibility to choose them. Your thoughts are a perfect mirror image of the norms and beliefs rooted inside your mind, but they are not your identity. At some point of your life, you have adopted some system of ideas that shaped your thoughts. You always have a chance to change this system of inadequate ideas that give rise to negative thoughts.

The paradox that comes into play here is that this normally is an inverse process. Only by driving away your negative thoughts and replacing them by positive ones can you foster a new system of positive thoughts that would help you transform your life. So the first step is to identify the negative vibrations that are emitted constantly by your brain:

Thoughts are a vital tool to change the reality that you experience.
Marty Vernadoe Dow

One way to express our thoughts is through self-talk. Words summarize our state of mind and humour, make us aware of our state of mind and inevitably reaffirm it. These words are the best way to anchor negative thoughts in our minds and are the first thing we have to reject as if they are maleficent spells that we direct at ourselves. Christian H. Godefroy, an expert in mental dynamics has elaborated an excellent list of mental sentences like, I cannot, I should not, it is going to be a failure, I am not lucky, I am always at fault, it is not for me, I am too old, I was never successful, why would I have it now, no one loves me... Godefroy's recipe includes changing these thoughts to positive affirmations like *I can, I must, I will win, I am lucky, I am going in the right direction, I am still young, I am pleasant to be with, I am worth a lot,* etc. Perhaps you are wrong if this seems to you just a way to fortify your self-esteem. Without faith in yourself, you will not be able to reach anywhere - a positive thought is more than just a simple ego massage.

RECOGNIZE YOUR NEGATIVE THOUGHTS BY YOUR SELF-TALK.

The Indian thinker and reiki expert, Anil Bhatnagar recommends similar techniques to transform negative thoughts into positive ones. His first advice is not to be trapped by negative thoughts; in the beginning it is very natural and normal for this to occur. What you must do then is to stop pursuing the activity immediately and clear up your mind or simply distract yourself with something else for a few minutes. Then restart the process of thought analysis with the attitude of an objective observer. Bhatnagar develops this idea in the following way:

> *Do not allow your thoughts to perturb you. Do not condemn or justify them. Do not try to control them. Only observe them. After some time, you will be able to identify and recognize your negative thoughts. Then, concentrate on replacing them with positive thoughts in a way that helps you develop a more positive attitude on that subject.*

Your friend, the Sun

If you find it difficult to replace or eliminate negative thought, you can apply the following technique recommended by Bhatnagar: Imagine the sun radiating a bright light. Use its imaginary rays to destroy your negative thoughts as soon as you detect them. Consider the sun like a constant and alert weapon that will hunt down negative thoughts and eliminate them with a ray and immediately withdraw. Do not forget to imagine that your imaginary sun is your loyal friend, always attentive of your desires.

It is recommended to maintain a kind of diary for your mind where you can note down the list of thoughts that have crossed your mind through the day. It will be helpful to remember what you have said during a conversation, what you have thought about your self or the images and ideas that have come to you spontaneously. According to Bhatnagar, it is very important to note down and analyze the conversations that you have had, the thoughts surrounding you while speaking, discussing, in meetings, etc. Was it essential? What was its motive? Did the conversation serve its goal? If not, why not? Did you use precise, appropriate, adequate and positive words? Did you feel satisfied or comfortable after this conversation?

Of course, you can formulate the same questions about the thoughts and reflections, spontaneous or otherwise, that crossed your mind throughout the day. This Hindu master recommends figuring out if it is possible to find ways to improve your thoughts while thinking

Exercises to develop attention

- *In the street.* Stop in a corner, observe the buildings opposite and choose one. Observe it at length, from the main door to the roof, check if there are shops in the ground floor, count the number of floors, windows or balconies and discover if it has some ornamental objects (grilles, plants, flowers, domestic objects, etc.), scrutinize architectonical details - the moulds of the facade, the shape and size of the door, etc. Then close your eyes and try to reconstruct the building mentally.
- *Listening to music.* It does not matter where you listen to music, be it at a live concert, a recording or even on radio. Nor does the genre selected matter. What is important is that there are various performers and that the listening could last between five and seven minutes. Choose an instrument and focus totally on listening to it throughout the number - for example, the bass in a jazz song, the violincello in a symphony or the battery in a rock concert.
  This activity will help you develop your audio attention that can play a very important role in concentration and visualization.
- *Watching a match.* It could be of any sport (football, basketball, hockey, handball, etc.). Pay attention to an individual player - the general development of the game should not interest you much. Follow him or her constantly, whether he or she moves or remains motionless. We do not have to judge his or her efforts but should not let our attention slip from the individual for even a second.
  Try to maintain this activity for ten to fifteen minutes and keep increasing the time carefully in later sessions.

These are only examples of exercises recommended in schools and mind study centres. You are free to adopt others that suit your lifestyle and circumstances better, the condition being that you must be able to practise the exercise with ease at any time, twice or thrice a day.

about someone or while indulging in a conversation. And he insists upon doing it immediately without leaving it for an analysis later.

Analyze your thoughts without identifying yourself with them, as an impartial observer.

Anil Bhatnagar

Overcome your fears

Fear is our body's natural reaction; it is a powerful biological reaction against risk or danger, real as well as imaginary. Fear is a primary defence and survival mechanism that helps us avoid danger or escape from it. The presence of fear is an important advantage if the threat is real, but totally negative if the danger is baseless.

The most frequent consequences of fear are anxiety that exasperates our nervous system, with the possibility of it deteriorating into depressive mania if it persists. In a majority of cases, the factors that unleash this kind of reaction are unreal or exaggerated and certainly not as serious as we imagine them to be. We weaken our resistance to negative thoughts and our health by allowing them to invade us. In fact, they can become the main mental barrier against beneficial and positive thoughts.

In the seventeenth century, William Shakespeare, who had great intuitive power and psychological sensibility, put in the words of one of his characters: "I am fearful of your fear".

One of the biggest global best-sellers on this topic is *"Feel the Fear and Do it Anyway"* by the American psychologist, Susan Jeffers. She confesses in the introduction that she was herself an extremely fearful person when she was young.

"I was constantly ruled by fear when I was young. Thus, it must not be surprising when I say that for a long part of my life, I was anchored to many things that did everything but favour me. My problem was the incessant voice that continuously nagged me saying that: 'It will be better not to change the situation; this is not your cup of tea; you will never do it for yourself; do not take risks; you could commit an error... You will regret it!'"

If you identify with the young Susan, you would be well aware that you will need to strive hard to liberate yourself from the bonds of the fear that stop your mind from accepting change. Jeffers does not want us to overcome fear but to recognize it, analyze its causes and the negative thoughts that provoke it. As the expressive title of the book suggests, she wants us to learn to live with fear, to accept it in order to be able to confront it.

Some one said that war heroes do what they do because it is no longer possible for them to tolerate their fears. Susan Jeffers does not agree with an inopportune reaction but a conscious process of re-educating our own mind:

> *Although the inability to confront fear might appear and feel like a psychological imbalance, it does not happen in the majority of cases. I think it is simply an educational problem, and by re-educating the mind, one can accept the fear as just a simple fact of life rather than as an obstacle to success.*

The faith in this conviction made Doctor Jeffers take up reading, attend educational workshops and hold discussions with scholars. Following the suggestions and advice she received, she describes a method she used to unlearn the thoughts that used to make her give up in the face of her insecurities. According to her, she started seeing the world as a less threatening and happier place and could experience the feeling of love for the first time in her life.

THE SECRET IS TO ACCEPT THE FEAR AND DO THINGS ALL THE SAME.

According to Jeffers' system, fear is felt at three levels. The fears at each level can be divided into two categories: fear of things that occur and fear of things that demand action from the individual. Let us see a list of both, necessarily incomplete:

Level one fears

Things that occur:
- Ageing
- Disability
- Retirement
- Solitude
- Kids leaving home
- Natural catastrophes
- Economic crisis
- Change
- Death
- Attacks, violence
- Disease, accident
- Loss of loved ones
- Robbery
- Rape

Things that demand action:
- Decision-making
- Change of job or profession
- Making new friends
- Going back to school
- Starting or ending a relationship

- Talking on the phone
- Weight loss
- Being interviewed
- Talking in public
- Driving automobiles
- Having sexual relations
- Committing an error

One of the most insidious characteristics of fear is that it tends to pervade many areas of our life. For example, if we are scared of making new friends, it is logical that we are also scared of going to parties, looking for a job, having sex, etc. The picture becomes clearer if we observe the list of second level fears. These fears are not related to specific situations; instead it involves the subject's intrinsic personality. Let us see some of these fears pointed out by Susan Jeffers:

Level two fears

- Fear of rejection
- Fear of failure
- Fear of success (more frequent than imagined)
- Fear of one's own vulnerability
- Fear of feeling deceived
- Fear of impotence
- Fear of disapproval
- Fear of loss of image

Level three fears

For Jeffers, this level has **only one** category that includes all. The creator of all fears is the fear or inability to confront and control fear.

Thus the only kind of third level fear is the following:

- I cannot help it!

In other words, I cannot stand solitude; I cannot accept the fact of growing old; I cannot confront failure; I cannot confront the responsibility of success...

The base of each one of your fears is just the fear.

Susan Jeffers

To confront all your fears is not to control the external aspects of a situation. You cannot manipulate the attitudes and actions of the external world towards you. You cannot defeat fear by controlling what your partner, kids, friends, boss or colleagues say or do. You cannot overcome your fears by imagining what would happen in an interview, in an exam, in the new job or what would happen to your money. You will just increase your anxiety by indulging in these thoughts because these are the aspects totally beyond your control. Let them take their own course and you will experience an enormous relief. Let us read one last quote by Susan Jeffers:

The only thing that you can do to control fear is to trust in your ability to confront all that comes your way. If you convince yourself that you will be able to deal successfully with whatever comes your way, what would be left to fear? Obviously, the answer to this question is: Nothing!

YOU MUST NOT TRY TO DEFEAT FEAR BY CONTROLLING EXTERNAL FACTORS.

Psychologists James and Constance Messina, have devoted more than three decades to the study of the effects of fear and its influence on different aspects of our life. They have dealt with numerous cases using their own technique based on the principles of inductive psychology. Basically, they focus on objectifying the fears, for example, by daily recording a person's feelings to later check which ones were more constant and repetitive and what were the circumstances of its recurrence.

Once you have recorded or identified the most active and constant fears of your life, you must undertake a process of classification and analysis that Messina describes step by step:

Step one

After having listed your fears, put them in decreasing order, putting the one that affects you the most first.

Step two

After classifying the fears according to their intensity, analyze your levels of motivation to fight against each of them, answering, in writing, the following questions:
- How real are these fears for me?
- How did they affect my past or present attitudes in life?
- How do they make me determine my own image, conception and self esteem?
- How do they weaken me?
- How do they inhibit me?
- What emotions block my thought process?
- How long have I been having these fears?
- Am I really convinced that I want to get rid of them?

Step three

Once you have analyzed your motivation level to fight these fears, convince yourself of the need of doing so. On a separate sheet of paper respond to the following questions:

- How do these fears influence you at the time of decision-making?
- How do they exacerbate your sense of insecurity?
- How do they prevent you from making changes in your life?
- How do they influence you at the time of accepting help from others?
- Till what point do these fears keep you tied up in yourself and away from others?
- How have they affected your education, work and professional goals?
- Do they contribute to the self-destructive feelings in you?

Step four

Once you have defined and catalogued the influence of fear in your life, go back to the original list and be ready to confront yourself with each one of the fears, one by one, starting from the one strongly rooted in your mind and which is the most harmful.

Step five

In order to drive away these fears, make use of the system that we have named "stop"; the process is explained below:

"Stop the fear" Method

 It is necessary to make a recording in a CD or a cassette to do these exercises. Record the world *'stop'* in intervals of one, two, three minutes and repeat the same series (1, 2, 3; 1, 2, 3, etc.) for as long as thirty minutes.

- Sit or lie in a relaxed position. Concentrate on the fear that you want to overcome, and play the recording; interrupt this thought every time you hear the word *stop* and start concentrating on it again till the next *stop*. If at any point you are disturbed or are unable to do it, repeat the whole process from the beginning. Do this activity every night at least for two weeks.
- You must be able to check the negative thought on hearing *stop* in two weeks time (if not, keep doing the exercise for one more week). Now you no longer need this external help. Concentrate on the negative thought or the thought or the situation that provokes fear in you, and clean it up just by pronouncing the word *stop* in a loud and firm voice. Repeat this activity daily for at least a fortnight.
- Once you are able to reject a negative thought in a loud voice, try doing so silently or in a soft tone. Do it every day for half an hour for a fortnight.
- Now you will practise true mental control of that particular fear without the help of any sound. Concentrate on the fear and then rub it off by pronouncing mentally the word *stop*. You shall be able to drive the fear off in a fortnight's time through positive mental energy that provokes the word *stop* when your being is invaded by a negative thought.
- Once you have seen the fruits of these efforts, and if you have

defeated the strongest of your fears, it will be a lot easier to reject the other weaker ones. Practice this activity on each one of your fears following the steps and recommended time limits.
- It is possible that once removed, one or more of these fears might try to re-enter your mind. In such cases, repeat the exercise as soon as possible against this particular fear in order to protect the positive thoughts that will be bringing important changes to your life.

Fear is illusory... it cannot live. Courage is eternal... it cannot die.
Sri Swami Sivananda

Rehearse visualization

The objective of all the techniques explained so far is to develop the ability to visualize, an ability that you must learn and master. It involves expressing positive thought in images - in other words, bring to mind the images that best represent the desires and ambitions that you hope to achieve with the Law of Attraction of cosmic energies. This involves creating a concrete image and reflecting it repeatedly in your thoughts, as if your brain was a projector and a screen.

It is fundamental not to visualize something you want to change from your present mental state. The secret lies in repeatedly imagining the change as having been accomplished, trying to add content and detail to it. For example, do not even think of your timidity if you want to overcome it. Instead, visualize yourself in the centre of a big gathering, boldly making interesting conversation with someone you like.

Of course educating, disciplining and training our imagination so that it concentrates only on positive thoughts is not an easy job that can be mastered in a day or two. The German psychologist Peter Kummer, whom we have already talked about in the section that deals with deep concentration, encourages us not to be disappointed:

I have never said that it is easy to get rid of the thoughts stacked for years and years; thoughts that are negative and dominated by fear. But if you persist in your efforts you will realize improvement within just a few weeks. You will be seeing things with a lot more optimism and this will make you realize that your life can change.

Visualization is the nexus that joins the spiritual and the physical worlds.

Peter Kummer

Of course, you must have faith in the positive effects of visualization for it to bear fruit - faith in the fact that your mind can create real situations and attract what you desire. This will help you attain unsuspected power. As Kummer says:

"Suddenly your habits and fears will no longer be able to interfere with your mind. The images of your visualizations will be clear and firm, they will eventually end up becoming a part of your daily life. You will realize that you possess a big force within yourself".

YOU MUST PERSIST WITH FAITH AND MUST SHOW ENOUGH PATIENCE TO ATTAIN THE BIG FORCE.

Visualization practice can be supported by certain techniques prescribed by Kummer. To affirm faith in positive energy and support your mental images, it is useful to practise affirmations like the following:

I love myself the way I am.
I am happy just because I am alive.
I enjoy my life.
I am full of energy.
I have good physical and mental health.
I am going to succeed in my efforts.
I am quiet and relaxed.
I always have time for myself.
I feel better every day.
My emotional relations are harmonious.
I think that abundance is part of my life.
I fully enjoy what I do.

Do not practise these assertions while trying to visualize. Do them all alone, repeating them in a loud voice and, if possible, in front of a mirror.

POSITIVE AFFIRMATIONS CAN FACILITATE THE VISUALIZATION PROCESS FOR THE FULFILLMENT OF YOUR ASPIRATIONS.

Visualization has an efficiency directly proportional to your ability to separate your senses from the external world and concentrate on the internal reality. If you can turn your concentration inwards, you will be able to create a mental image that stimulates your physical and psychological being. The image will automatically come as soon as you concentrate your willpower and attention on your inner self, getting rid of the exterior world.

The last paragraph is by Doctor Gerald Epstein, who specializes in preventing and curing diseases through positive visualization. Epstein recommends the posture of the Pharaoh in order to disconnect your senses from the external world. The posture of the Pharaoh means to sit straight on a chair with a straight back, rest with hands supported on the arm rests with palms facing upwards, sidewards or downwards. The feet must touch the floor uniformly. You must avoid crossing your arms and legs during the process of visualization; keep them away from other parts of the body. According to Epstein, our sensorial consciousness maintains itself isolated from external messages in this physical position; it also aids the search for internal principles, an internal guide that counsels us before taking any decision. This position also helps us maintain deep breathing and attention, while a lying down position induces sleep.

A royal posture

The posture of the Pharaoh originates from the position adopted by the Egyptian Pharaohs and high profile leaders. The common man in old times used to sit on the floor while the dignitaries used to sit in a chair or a throne. Later, kings and emperors maintained this posture above the rest of the people when they were acting as judges in a legal process, when they had to resolve an important matter or maintain protocol on important occasions. From the Pharaoh Kefren to the Persian king Dario, from the celebrated statue of Abraham Lincoln in Washington DC to an astronaut's position in his spacecraft; the posture of the Pharaoh has always been a sign of supreme power and control over a situation.

The ability to visualize is not attained by just desiring it, but after constant and patient training over a period of time that could be very long. We must underline that this ability, and the time and effort required to attain it, vary a lot from individual to individual. There are some who are capable of attaining it within no time and some who encounter a series of difficulties in mastering it.

Of course the ability to visualize broadly depends on the previous practice of exercises like correct breathing, relaxation and concentration control. But still, it is possible that you find it difficult to visualize scenes with which you want to work. Doctor Epstein offers some advice to improve your ability to visualize:

- Observe for around three minutes a photograph or a painting depicting a landscape. Then close your eyes and try to visualize the image.
- Remember with your eyes open some pleasant scene from your earlier years. Then close your eyes and try visualizing it.
- In the same way, use your non-visual senses like smell, taste, sound and touch. All our senses produce mental stimulations that can help you visualize an image related with this stimulus.

What you cannot do in the beginning is to forcefully visualize a concrete image; something which is achieved only after a lot of practice. Epstein recommends a more patient attitude:

Generally, while trying to improve your visualization skills, make an effort to be relaxed, breathe deeply three times, close your eyes and then, wait for the visualization. Let the image come by itself. And when it comes, accept it. Whatever image emerges, it is adequate and can be useful, although it may appear to be absurd and useless.

IN THE BEGINNING, VISUALIZATION DEMANDS PATIENCE, MODESTY AND ACCEPTANCE OF IMPERFECT IMAGES.

The English metaphysicist Ursula Markham is greatly recognized in her country as well as abroad thanks to her numerous books. She describes a method which she calls "visualizations to live", whose wide range of topics include psychic traumas that result in anguish, depression or phobias, to stopping smoking or quitting biting one's nails.

All of us have something within us that we would like to change.
Ursula Markham

Like her colleagues, Markham accords prime importance to the ability to be relaxed and also to the use of a specific recording or a story to stimulate visualization appropriate to achieve our objectives:

Visualizations are simply what they appear to be: a series of scripts or arguments created to help you to improve, whatever the problems that you might have now or in the future. You can make someone else read them to you or you yourself can read them in a loud voice, recording it at the same time.

Thus, the process of visualization would be:

- *See:* see the written words when you read them loudly.
- *Speak:* pronounce the words in order to record them.
- *Listen:* listen to these words once recorded.
- *Imagine:* convert these words into mental images while listening to your recorded voice.

Obviously the key to visualization lies in the fourth and the last step. Problems related to adult life like studies, family, work, money, etc., occupy most of our thoughts and intrude into our efforts at abstraction. We slowly start losing the ability to imagine, something we enjoyed a lot during our childhood but which now lies inactive and completely passive in the substrata of our mind. If we are suddenly asked to imagine a beautiful lake in paradise, most probably we achieve only a very poor, partial or unstable image that is mixed with other thoughts that preoccupy us more. Or we might not be able to achieve visualization at all.

Markham is aware of this problem and suggests a method to overcome it:

> *Let us suppose that you are the kind of person who finds it very difficult to create visual images. What can you do to improve it? Try thinking of imagination as a muscle, and, like any other muscle, it loses power if you do not exercise it. And, like any other muscle, it cannot be exercised infrequently in the hope that it will remain robust over a period of time. It must be used every day, slowly enhancing its power and force.*

Markham's method to optimize imagination

First step

- Write down on a piece of paper the following list of words: house, tree, tomato, cow, baby, sea, chair, narcissist, telephone and teapot.
- Read these words one by one loudly. Every time you read a word, close your eyes and visualize what it represents. Irrespective of achieving it, carry on to the next word till reaching the end.

Second step

Once you master the first step, nourish your imagination by thinking up scenes for visualization. It can be any scene that you know well and that you like to visualize. The following are some examples:
- your childhood bedroom;
- the interior of any room of your house;
- a place where you have spent pleasant vacations.

Third step

Now you need to add some action to the scenes you visualize in order to rehearse seeing yourself fulfilling your desires. Avoid anything that is difficult or disturbing for you. Limit yourself to pleasant and simple activities. Here are some examples, but you can substitute them with any other activity you may prefer:

- walking down a known route, observing the environment;
- going up a part of stairs;
- cooking some dish;
- indulging in your favourite pastime.

You must practise this system daily, dedicating at least one week to each activity before moving on to the next. You should verify that your ability to visualize a scene improves progressively over the period you exercise each script.

TRAIN YOUR IMAGINATION TO BE ABLE TO IMPROVE AND OPTIMIZE YOUR VISUALIZATIONS.

Exercising your willpower, consistency in your efforts and perseverance in following this simple technique will help you master visualization. This will be the moment to start with your transformation plan. All experts recommend that you apply the visualization technique to all aspects of life like health, relationships, finances, success, job or creativity.

A life that is not analyzed is not worth living.
Plato

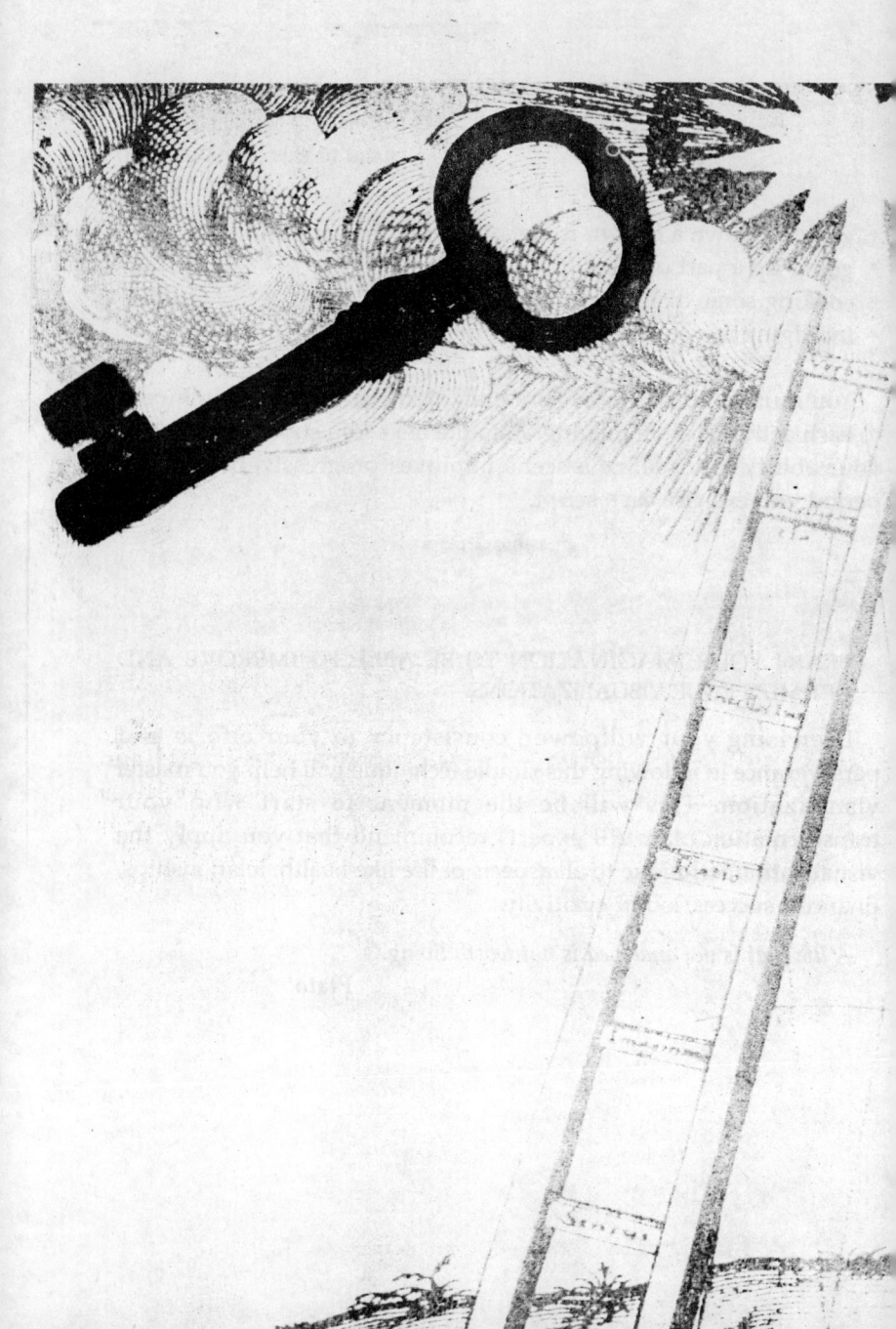

4.

How can you transform your life?

*Confidently move towards your dreams,
in order to live the life you have imagined.*
Henry David Thoreau

Your aim now is to transform your current existence into a better and more satisfied life. If you have carefully read the previous sections, if you agree with the concepts explained there, if you consciously have followed the practical advice and if you feel yourself capable of creative visualization, you can start working towards a better life from this moment itself.

Most probably there are various areas of your life that you want to modify or improve: attain spiritual peace; overcome the phobias and traumas of your mind, be it serious or not so serious; attain and maintain good physical health; enjoy the affection that your companions, your family and friends offer to you; be respected and appreciated by your boss and colleagues; achieve the success you want in your professional life; ensure long-term economic well-being; and other legitimate and reasonable ambitions that till now you have not been able to fulfil.

This book will keep assisting you in the process of change that you are going to undertake, with the help of the great masters of the past and present. For this reason, we have divided our advice according to topics or different areas of life, linking them to the normal desires that most people have under each of these.

We advise you to read all sections even if your main objective is centred in one of them. For example, if you want that someone reciprocate your love, you will find the relevant advice in the section "Improve your love life". But the content of this section will be of greater utility if you study other related topics too, like for example those included in the section "Attain spiritual harmony and mental equilibrium". We hope that in this way, our help will prove more practical and efficient. But remember that the responsibility is all yours, just as will be the achievements at the end of the journey along the path to transformation.

YOU MUST VISUALIZE ALL THE THINGS THAT YOU DESIRE TO CHANGE IN YOUR LIFE.

Achieve spiritual harmony and mental equilibrium.

If we ask someone what his or her primary desire is, the answer will be as simple as: "I want to be happy". This answer transcends age, gender, ethnicity or geography. It is difficult to define happiness, and philosophers, thinkers and psychologists themselves have not been able to agree upon an exact description of the sentiment called happiness. For a few, it is exclusively something they experience in special and brief moments like achieving some success, a passionate love affair, childbirth, the solution of a serious problem and other favourable and remarkable occurrences in life. The possibility of a totally happy existence does not exist from this point of view given that the journey of life is full of happy and sad patches, of successes and failures, of love and hate, of enthusiasm and anguish.

Nevertheless, since man became conscious of his existence, he looked for the lost paradise where happiness ruled and tried to find it through religion or through wisdom - in other words, through faith or knowledge. In the best of cases, it is the combination of these two that can lead us to happiness.

4. HOW CAN YOU TRANSFORM YOUR LIFE

All humans aspire for the divine and the master must help him to invoke the divinity that is within him.

Swami Vivekananda

We have said that the search for long-lasting happiness is based upon two principles: faith and knowledge. Let us now see why:

- *Faith:* Having faith in the kindness and justice of God (whatever be the name and appearance we might assign to Him), in His expression through cosmic energies and in the forces that lie secretly in our mind. This certainty must sustain your faith in yourself and also your desire for change towards a better life.
- *Knowledge:* Having knowledge regarding the possibilities of your mind and also about your attitudes and the techniques of activating these possibilities; also knowledge of how to make them work through visualization and affirmations. This knowledge will help you exploit and optimize necessary mental resources so that your desire for change materializes.

Existential happiness is based on spiritual harmony and a healthy and long lasting mental equilibrium. Although here we display it as two different entities, in fact they are two faces of the same coin and are intimately linked, so much so that one cannot be achieved without the other.

According to the teachings of Swami Vivekananda, a master of the Vedas, "every man must be treated not according to what he shows as evident but to what his aspirations are". He adds:

> *Every individual is potentially divine. Your objective is to evoke this internal divinity by controlling your internal and external nature. Do this through work, worship, mind control or through philosophical discourse – follow one or more or all these paths and attain freedom. This is what our religion means. (...) The doctrines, dogmas, rituals, books, temples and images are only secondary details.*

If you go deep down, you will find Unity between individuals, races, rich and poor, high and low, gods and humans, humans and animals. If you go deeply enough, all will be seen as just a variation of the One, and the one who has achieved this concept of unity does not need illusions. What can deceive him? He knows the reality of all, the secret of all,..; Where can misery exist for him? He has followed the path of reality towards the Master, the Centre, the Unity of all which is the Eternal Existence, Eternal Knowledge, Eternal Happiness.

The universe is ready to reveal its secrets only if we know how to "hit" correctly. The intensity and the force of this "hit" depend on our concentration. There is no limit to the potential of the human mind.

Thought is the propulsive force in us. Fill your mind up with the most elevated thoughts, hear them day after day and think about them month after month. You must never mind failures, they are natural. These failures are the beauty of life.

There must be meditation. Meditation is essential. Meditate! Meditation is the best approach to a spiritual life. That is the moment when we no longer are material, when the soul is thinking about itself, when we are free of all material worry..., this is the marvellous moment when we are in touch with our Soul.

WITH TRUE FAITH, THERE IS NO LIMIT TO THE POWER OF THE HUMAN MIND.

The loss of our spiritual dimension seriously worries Susan Jeffers, who talks about this problem in one of the most inspired chapters of her book *Feel the Fear and Do it Anyway*:

> *Very often we hear the expression "body, mind and soul" to define the totality of our existence. Current society is concerned primarily about the body and the mind. The spiritual side of us containing awareness of our Superior self has been gradually lost and no one knows how. There are a very small number of places where something about the Superior being within us is taught. The fact that we have concentrated only upon the intellectual and physical side must not surprise us. Some of us do not even know about the existence of the spiritual side at all.*

In the above, the author explains one of the most interesting theories about mental powers. It talks about the existence of a superior us, something very powerful that remains hidden within but of which we are not conscious. Unlike Freud's "super ego", the "superior us" does not repress or control our primary impulses, but it acts as a great source of energy that seems to be in reserve for decisive moments of our life. This powerful force works only at an appropriate moment, without our conscious permission and without having been called for.

By talking about the actions of the "superior us", Jeffers means those actions performed by some people that seem to be phenomenal. She cites the example of the head of a family who, in desperation, lifts up alone a car under which his wife and kids were trapped; and later on does not understand the source of the strength that enabled him to do it.

"I do not know how I did it but I did it" is how the protagonist of the heroic deed explains it. And it indeed is true that his conscious mind does not know how he actually accomplished this miracle, this unexplainable, extraordinary prodigious task that only a divine soul can undertake. For Jeffers, this is a manifestation of the divine component that exists in all of us.

When we are far from our "superior us", we feel what Roberto Assagiolio so adequately defined as "divine nostalgia". When we have the sensation of being lost, of no longer following our own path, what we should do is find again the road towards home. Simply, use the tools that show us the way towards the "superior us"... and in this way, let positive sentiments flow.

I think that we are really looking for the divine essence that is in all of us.

Susan Jeffers

Make the "loquacious" keep quiet

According to Susan Jeffers, there are two fundamental forces inside our mind. We are already familiar with the existence of the "superior us", powerful and positive, but which is not always present in our conscious mind. Very often, our conscious mind is occupied by another force that emits negative and contradictory messages that tend to confuse, terrorize ordepressus. Jeffers calls this dangerous mental messenger "garrulous" because of its never ending chatter and gloomy and deceitful nature. "It is the sediment of all our negative conditioning, since our birth till the present", she says. "It contains our childhood ego that demands constant attention but does not know how to give attention. The conscious sends to the subconscious mind orders based upon information that it receives either from the "superior us" or the "loquacious". We can train our mind to receive information from the one or the other".

WE MUST GIVE PRIORITY TO THE POSITIVE MESSAGES THAT OUR "SUPERIOR US" SENDS TO THE CONSCIOUS MIND.

The achievement of individual peace and happiness is considered very different in Western and Oriental cultures. We, in the West, understand this term in a very pragmatic sense, through attaining determined personal goals like success, love and admiration, good health and the enjoyment of assured and legitimate financial well-being whereas in the East, they look for the elevation of the spirit through rejection of the material and enlightenment of the spiritual.

This difference has not stopped the great figures of positive thought in America and Europe from accepting, admiring and practising many of the principles and norms of Oriental religions and philosophies, especially those belonging to Hinduism and Buddhism. It can be observed that the various techniques of breathing, relaxing and concentrating owe a lot to Asian spiritual traditions. Both these worlds are different when it comes to meditation and visualization.

For the Western mentalists, meditation means continuous concentration on an issue or its visualization. However, for the spiritual masters of Hinduism, meditation is exactly the opposite of fixing one's attention on one point exclusively. For them, it means to open up the mind, to get rid of any image and thought, to allow neutral spaces among thoughts. The result is access to mental calm, peaceful spiritual quietness that stimulates union with the divine, like the contemplative life in Christian mystical tradition.

However, Ayurveda does not ignore an individual's relation with the world that surrounds him or her, and proposes a technique of meditation and visualization to achieve some worldly objectives too. The basic idea is to plan out a strategy before embarking on any action. Such strategy or plan means fixing up a series of objectives for oneself in order to achieve one's goals. All our actions have some consequence, this consequence must be good, be it for ourselves or for others.

A man is what he desires in his heart.
Ayurveda

Whatever the mystical or philosophical leanings, there are a series of techniques of visualization that are common to all. These are as follows.

The surroundings

As in Western tradition, the best surroundings to practise meditation is in a tranquil, nicely ventilated place that has plenty of natural light. It is a common practice in the East to create a favourable atmosphere by hanging in the room material related to contemplation like images, icons, candles, sacred books, luminous spheres or in the case of Buddhism, translucent statues of Buddha.

The posture

The physical position has a special relevance in traditional Oriental meditation techniques. The most comfortable of all is that of the lotus, with legs crossed on the ground, with the feet on the thighs and the trunk straight. We have already referred to the posture of the Pharaoh, of Egyptian origin and recommended it to those who want to meditate

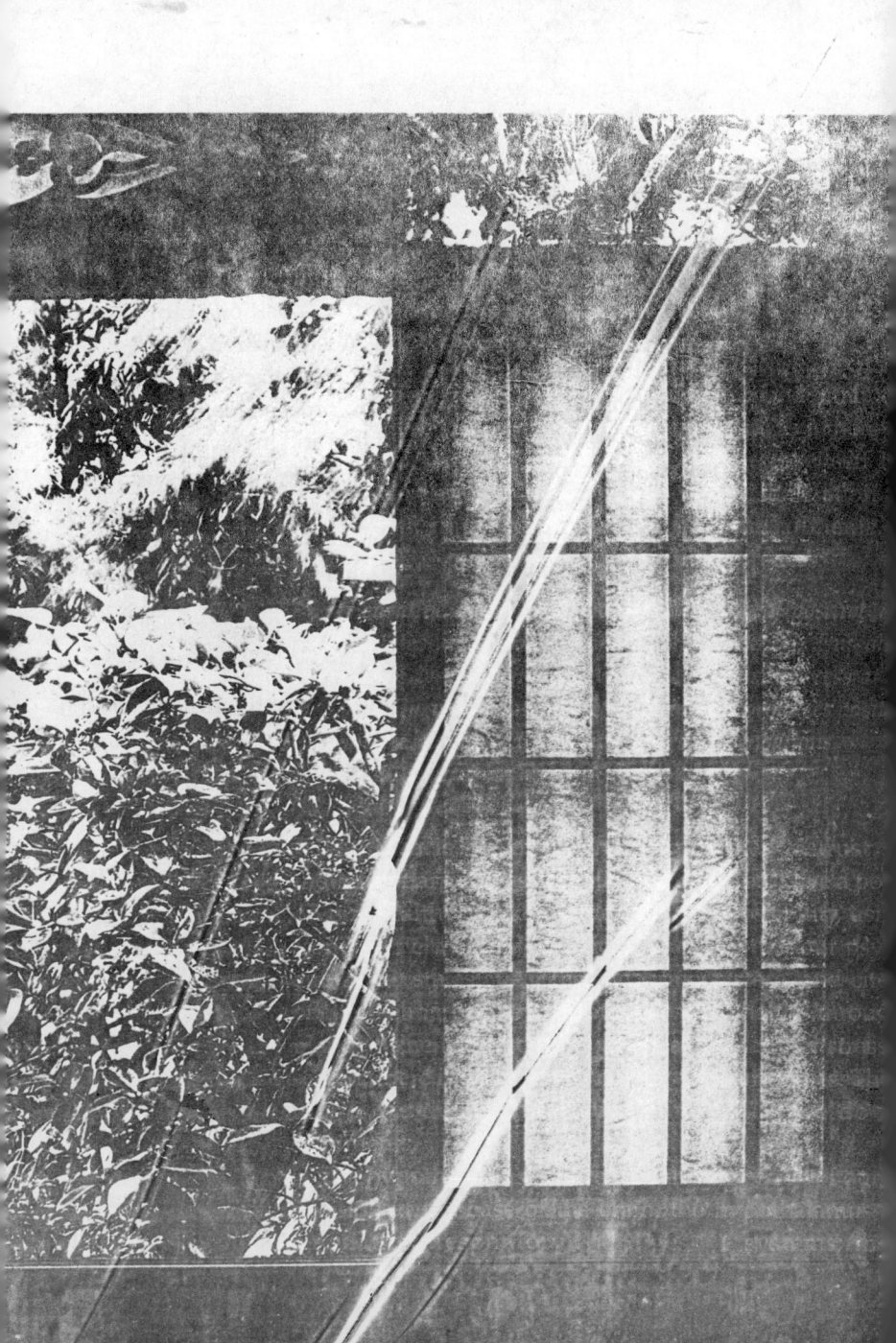

sitting in a chair. Other classic postures are: positions of Hatha Yoga prescribed by Patanjali in the *yoga Sutras*; positions proposed by Buddhism, which is very popular in the West; position of the *kum nye* method from Tibet; position of the *gurdieff* movement or position with the feet embracing an imaginary column, practised by the Taoists.

Most of these postures are uncomfortable and involve a certain risk for the novice; it is recommended to practise these postures under the vigilance of an expert. The common feature in all of them is maintaining a straight back and vertebral column, a position that is believed to favour meditation and visualization.

The sources of help

Often, Oriental methods use rituals to induce the desired mental state for meditation. For example, aromatic vegetable oils, sacred water ablutions, flower or incense offerings that clean the mind and help in concentration and stimulate psychic energies that help in meditation.

There are elements that help meditation, like the mantras in Hindu meditation techniques. One of these widely used mantras is the syllable OM, pronounced with a vibrating M sound. Some other syllables or words exist too generally taken from the Sanskrit language. Buddhists, on the other hand, help themselves during meditation by controlling the rhythm of their breathing, be it diaphramatic or deep breathing.

The personal attitude

The most favourable attitude to practise meditation is to become a receptive observer. Try observing your own internal mind, alternating this with a contemplation of support elements without concentrating on anything in particular. Notice how your mind is getting cleaned from any thought till it remains totally empty like a blank paper. Only then will you be able to draw the mental images that you wish.

The time

Deep meditation must be practised every day and the best results are obtained by performing it twice a day. The ideal time for each session is one hour, although beginners can do it for half an hour and can keep increasing the duration as they gain mastery over the technique.

> *Life is what it is, you cannot change it, but you can certainly change yourself.*
>
> **Hazrat Hinayat Khan**

Use of curative visualization

The assumed separation between the body and the mind (the *soma* and the *psiquis* of the Greeks) has its origin in the traditional division between the flesh and the soul or between two ideas totally different, even opposite, in their essence. Today we know that both are interdependent and form one indivisible unit that constitutes the individual, that is, each one of us.

The mind-body equilibrium is a fundamental factor for our physical well-being. If one of them becomes unstable, it will affect the other. This is the concept that led ancient physiologists to refer to an angry person as a bilious character. The Latin sentence "mens sana in corpore sano" expresses the same sentiment. Today, medical science accepts the existence of psychosomatic diseases and also confirms that certain organic or traumatic ailments affect the mental equilibrium of the patient.

Visualization is a powerful tool to enjoy good health through the mind.
Linda Mackenzie

The mutual influence between mind and body imbues visualization and positive thinking with special potential as a therapeutic practice. Apart from the fact that mental harmony by itself is a factor that stimulates our organic defense, specific visualization acts effectively to prevent, improve or cure our physical ailments. Doctor Linda Mackenzie explains the reasons for this process:

In curative treatments, the repetitive use of positive visualization facilitates access to the mind-body connection. This allows both of them to work together towards the curative process at the physical level. The visualization of positive images produces positive emotions that are manifested in positive physical sensations.

The idea is so simple that it provokes distrust. Can a simple thought, sharp and as repetitive as it may be, have a positive influence on our health? Mackenzie defends this possibility, using an example from the field of endocrinology. She says that our psychological and emotional states affect the endocrine system, and cites the example of the feeling of fear that produces adrenaline through our adrenal glands. When we are calm, or we are not under stress or we are not scared, there is no adrenaline release in our bodies. The reverse exists too: if we do not have adrenaline at all, we do not feel these sentiments.

The hypothalamus is the commanding centre of our body. From its position at the base of the brain, the hypothalamus controls blood circulation, respiratory and digestive systems; the adrenal and pituitary glands, body temperature and blood sugar level. Apart from these functions, it also accomplishes the exchange of emotions and sensations between the mind and the body through messenger hormones named neuropeptides. These chemical transmitters send messages from the brain to the rest of the body. The neuropeptides reach the principal zones of our immune system, making the body and mind work together to ensure good health.

ENDOCRINOLOGY ENDORSES THE THERAPEUTIC RELATION BETWEEN MIND AND BODY.

Praise for the right side of the brain

Linda Mackenzie is a follower of the controversial theory of the existence of "two brains", and she explains its importance in visualization in the following manner: "The brain is divided into two parts: the left or the logical brain that controls speech, knowledge, and rational thought; and the right brain which is creative, and dominates imagination and intuition and is the one that makes possible the mind-body connection that helps us achieve our goals. The right side of the brain automatically takes you towards your objective. It totally accepts what you want to attain, without expressing its opinion and acts to get it without prejudice. This is why visualization works with the right and the creative side of the brain, and not with the logical and rational left side".

Mackenzie offers several tips to optimize the visualization process. Following her advice should help you better in resolving your troubles or healing physical or psychic ailments:

1. *Define your objective with precision.* Your visualization must be centred upon the object of your desire. Remember that your body will react to the vibrations you emit. So when you visualize your objective, keep in mind that it should be:
- Clear
- Specific
- Reachable

And reassure yourself about what you feel, what you know and your faith in your ability to achieve your goal.

2. *Assume responsibility.* It has been proven that trying to visualize something without taking responsibility for it does not yield positive results. In order to visualize what you are looking for, you must assume responsibility and play an active role. If you practise visualization in the morning as well as in the evening, it will take six weeks to achieve the goal. There are people who seem to see results right from the beginning, but keep in mind that body and mind are different for different individuals, the time taken to and the way in which we process information are also different. So be patient and fulfil the following responsibilities:
- Be consistent with yourself.
- Be committed to yourself.
- Work on visualization regularly.
- Be patient and focused.
- Be mentally relaxed.
- Do not forget that a relaxed state of mind permits a direct access to your subconscious.

3. *Visualize correctly.* The therapeutic visualization process is a relatively simple one. Once you have defined the appropriate image, you must work on visualizing it in your mind:

- Concentrate on your objective and say it aloud.
- Close your eyes and imagine yourself enduring the treatment or imagine you are totally cured from your ailment.
- Observe how your body emits health to you.
- Feel the physical and mental well being.
- Be convinced that you are now healthy.

4. *Do not give up if you fail.* Use your imagination to visualize how your body cells are being cured or how your immune system fights against the invaders. You can also apply external resources like the following:

- Imagine yourself healthy and happy, in a very beautiful and serene environment.
- Try reading testimonies of visualization or books on self-hypnosis.
- Try recording a support guide, using your own voice.

The key to mental visualization lies in the ability to link emotions, sensations and images.

Gerald Epstein

Let us go back to the knowledge and experience of Doctor Epstein, to explore the deep therapeutic possibilities of visualization. In his books and articles, Doctor Epstein has reiterated several times that mental energy can cure or significantly improve many physical ailments:

Although Western medicine is reluctant to accept the concept that the mind can alter the body, it postulates that you must believe in just the opposite (that something physical can affect the mind) and use this link frequently. Tranquilizers, anti-depressives and

anesthetics are an example of it. Since it is obvious that the body can affect the mind, why is it so difficult to accept that mental powers like willpower or imagination can affect the physical body?

My clinical experience in the last fifteen years has provided me with lot of evidence, not only of the mind affecting the body but also evidence of the capacity of mental visualization to contribute to the body's treatment.*

Like all similar processes, therapeutic visualization, be it preventive or curative, means invoking or creating a mental image - in other words, an imaginary form connected to the physical object that will not stop being real within the individual's subjectivity. It has the same qualities as the object, thing or occurrence; it is also a form of matter in this world although without mass, volume or substance. To use modern phraseology, it is a virtual image that is the equivalent of what we can see and create in an abstract online network.

Besides, this virtual image has energy. Or, to say it differently, the virtual image extracts energy from our mind in order to produce vibrations corresponding to what the visualization represents. In turn, these vibrations can be mentally canalized towards the part of our body that needs to be cured. For example, if you suffer from cold, you can imagine your respiratory system (nose, throat, trachea, lungs, etc.) and "see" the mucus that obstructs the track, you can also visualize reducing the irritation and inflammation of the tissues till they recover their normal rhythm and until the fever disappears.

Of course that would not be happening in your physical body, at least in the moment of visualization, but if you consciously repeat the visualization, this recuperation process will be completed in a shorter

---

*Among the ailments and physical sickness that Epstein cured or helped to cure as a clinical doctor are rheumatic arthritis, prostate, ovarian tumours, breast cancer, skin rashes, haemorrhoids and conjunctivitis as recorded in his clinical diaries..

time than you initially expected. For this to happen effectively, it is convenient to follow Gerald Epstein's advice:

> *There are four aspects for the mind's preparation for a curative visualization. The first two constitute the whole exercise of visualization. I call these two elements "intention" and "tranquilization". The other two constitute the therapeutic visualization experience in its totality. I call them "washing" and "change".*

Now we offer you a summary of the text written by the author regarding the four elements in his work *Curative Visualization*:

Intention

Visualization is directly and actively related to the intention, that is, the mental action that directs our attention and our actions. The attention is the active expression of our desires, canalized through our physiological systems. It manifests itself through action be it physical or mental. In simple words: the intention is what we want to achieve.

What does it have to do with visualization and the treatment? When we practise visualization, we must always first define and clarify our intention. Thus, for example, if you want to treat a broken bone, before starting the exercise, you must tell yourself, perhaps aloud, that you are doing this visualization activity to rejoin this bone. We could consider it to be an internal instruction; a kind of computer programme for your mind with the aim to concentrate only on what it should work on. On telling yourself that you are going to perform a task with conviction, the chances of success improves.

Willpower is an intrinsic aspect of the intention; it depends upon the intention. Willpower is nothing else but an impulse or a vital force that prepares us to take decisions. Intention is the result of the direction we impose on our willpower. Thus, this is a directed willpower, and is fundamental for all the self-cure activity that is undertaken through visualization. Through its use, we direct the willpower towards ourselves in order to find new ways that lead us to better health and a more satisfactory life. Then we consciously start taking control of our life.

Tranquilization

The second requisite to prepare our mind for therapeutic visualization is what Epstein calls "tranquillization". The curative environment requires two types of calmness: the external and the internal. The first one helps us concentrate on the process of going deep within ourselves. Every day disturbances and noises can stop us from attaining this kind of concentration. Practising this does not mean to take refuge in a monastery or a cave, but it certainly implies being in a serene environment without any disturbance.

Serenity does not mean absolute silence. Certain kinds of noises can contribute to your internal tranquillity: the warble of a bird, the murmuring of rain or even the noise of far-off traffic. If you do not pay any special attention to these sounds, they will eventually become a part of your visualization process. If you put extra effort to get rid of these sounds, you will be busier getting rid of these distractions rather than concentrating on the visualization process.

Relaxation is the internal aspect of tranquillization. Even after having admitted this, Doctor Epstein warns that meditative or profound relaxation is not adequate in therapeutic exercises. Overdoing, as far as relaxation is concerned, might render you unconscious or drowsy and less receptive to the visualizing experience. Your objective is not to relax but to imagine and to remember. In any case, it is required to maintain adequate relaxation to be able to perform the visualization with tranquility and without stress.

THERAPEUTIC VISUALIZATION DEMANDS A CLEAR INTENTION AND CONSCIOUS AND TRANQUIL ATTENTION.

The other two aspects that Doctor Epstein underlines in his work on visualization for the purpose of treatment are the processes that he calls "wash" and "change". These are the elements that go much beyond the mere intention to cure a physical ailment or an organic dysfunction, as they come into direct contact with our values, conducts and habits. If we do not pay enough attention to them, all efforts through visualization will result in failure.

Washing

The author reminds us of the fact that the majority of the ancient medical knowledge, Eastern as well as Western, use the process of washing as a treatment process. We are referring to the therapeutic and ritualistic body wash, as it occurred in the Egyptian culture, in the Roman and Arab baths, in the rite of mikvah among the Jews, in European thermal places, and present-day spas. As far as religion is concerned, we know that Christian creeds use water in baptism as a symbol of washing the soul of the new believer, in some cases with complete immersion.

The relation between body and mind works only if both of them are "clean". This means the body should be washed and the mind at peace with itself. The sanitary virtues of body hygiene are well known and contribute to good mental health. The following statement by Gerald Epstein is based on this principle:

> *When I say that washing is necessary for the visualization process, I am of course, talking about something beyond physical hygiene. Without any intention to moralize, I would suggest that being healthy is the same as being clean, in all senses of the word. Talking in ethical terms, we must question ourselves on how clean we are when it comes to interacting with others. Many people consider regaining good health as part of their personal inheritance. However, they deceive*

themselves if they are incapable of seeing the relation between disease and improper conduct.

In each of us, all moral or ethical misconduct is registered by our body and can negatively influence our physical and mental life.

In short, in order to initiate our treatment process through mental energy, we must start by "washing our own acts". This cleansing act is part of a conscious and voluntary attitude that precedes the visualization process. It implies carefully scrutinizing ourselves internally, and being ready to listen to our body and emotions and to understand what they tell us. In Gerald Epstein's words:

Through the use of images, we can get rid of the negative feelings that suggest that something is wrong, correct our own errors and identify our own destructive tendencies. Later on, we will be able to confront our personal ailments and cure them. The process of washing is part of the process of treatment and both create a space so that new and healthy tendencies arise in order to cure the ailment.

Change

The fourth and last element of Doctor Epstein's proposal is change, not in the sense of transformation, but in the sense of accepting the constant changes that occur around us, and letting the course of life flow smoothly. Accepting change means a change in ourselves that makes us accept the mutable nature of things. He says that we have to accept the possibility of pain and suffering. Often, we believe that "positive thinking" involves denying the possibility of pain and suffering. This denial will result in creating exactly the kind of situation we want to avoid.

Sticking to a favourable situation believing that it will be permanent may create internal difficulties and tension that might find its expression in the form of bodily ailments. Psychoanalysis names this situation as "neurosis of conversion" which converts the psychic trauma or mental barrier into physical suffering. In Epstein's version it is expressed in the following way:

> *The visualization process in our mind and body is basically a process of liberating ourselves to become truly individual beings that can live harmoniously with any kind of change. On making ourselves capable of abandoning the physical world of objects and appearances, mental visualization helps us get rid of repressive attitudes and behaviours that frequently affect our health negatively.*
>
> *Intention, tranquilization, washing and change - these are the components of a healthy state of being. As you keep learning to use these components to cure you of your ailments and specific problems, you shall be transformed into not only a healthier person but also a freer one, ready to experiment with the infinite possibilities that life offers us.*

If your body and mind are healthy, you must start curing your soul.

Plato

Improve your love life

For a balanced and happy life, it is essential to be able to love and be loved. Since childhood, we are surrounded by our loved ones like parents, siblings, grandparents and other family members with whom we exchange affection at various levels. Soon we open up to a world of new relations like friends, fellow students, and perhaps some teachers. There could be other people with whom we share our affections. These affections are not always symmetric and it is possible that some times we may feel unloved by some member of our family or that our love is not reciprocated by someone. Similarly, we may not reciprocate the love expressed to us by other people.

All this comes into play unconsciously when we fall in love. The highest and also the most discordant kind of love is passionate love, understood as an obsession with an individual in whom we deposit all our appetite for affection. If the individual we love reciprocates, both are responsible for the relationship.. But if the loved one ignores or rejects us, it opens up an abyss that converts the very sentiment of love into an insubstantial and, therefore, an ineffective feature of our life.

As in other cases, most of the problems of love occur not because of others but because of the individuals themselves. It is our own negative thoughts, our low self-esteem or our self-destructive tendencies that keep us from appearing attractive and from adequately expressing our own personality. That unloved being is not your full personality. Within you, there is another being with immense faith in him/herself, and who knows to love and be loved - a being who can be revealed only by your own dormant mental energies.

Whatever life throws at us, it will be easier to confront if we feel loved.
Ursula Markham

We have already introduced the British therapist Ursula Markham. Let us get back to her in order to study the chapter dedicated to the problems of love in her book *The answers are Within You*:

Love, without any doubt, is one of the most positive emotions that can make us feel better physically as well as emotionally. There are various types of love, and all of them are important. Although it could be that we are not very fortunate to experience all kinds of love at the same time, they do exist around us and the more we give, the more it is possible that we receive in return.

Markham continues her advice pointing out that the love we receive should be expressed appropriately to elicit a similar response:

Despite knowing that people around us love us, if this love is not expressed, it becomes easy to doubt it when we have negative thoughts. Keeping this in mind, it is very important for us to remind others that we love them with words, hugs, paying attention to them and spending time with them.

Being an expert in the use of mental energies, Markham proposes visualization to ensure a healthy love life. Her text is reproduced below.

Visualization for love
(Ursula Markham)

While I relax, I let my mind to go back to my childhood and think about the love I used to feel then - perhaps the love I used to feel for my family, for a domestic animal, or even for a doll or a teddy bear. Then, it does not worry me at all whether or not this love is reciprocated. I love without any condition. I let this feeling of warm and soft love pervade my whole being. I continue to be the same person; I still have a lot of love to give to people.

I have also received love in my life: love of my parents, my family, my friends or that from a romantic relationship. Irrespective of these people not being by my side now, this love has not changed; it continues to be around me. I conserve the memory of their love that maintains this sensation of affection. There is no reason for those far away from me to stop loving me only because they cannot see me.

As I understand the importance of the knowledge that one is loved, I make sure that I always convey my feelings to those I love. I will tell them with words, I demonstrate my affection towards them with my gestures, always offering them my time and my attention. I do understand that the more love I give, the more I will receive in return.

I will never forget to love myself. It is an important though frequently forgotten form of love. I know that like other human beings, I too have my quota of defects. But we do not love only what is perfect. True love is given unconditionally ignoring defects. So I can love myself with all my imperfections because, thanks to this love, I will be able to work to change any aspect of my personality that I think is harmful to me.

"No matter what might happen to me, I will always keep a part of this love for myself and for others in reserve to take refuge in when needed. It will help me confront negative situations and avoid them".

The author suggests visualizing these thoughts along with the following affirmations:

- I know what to be loved is.
- I love myself.
- I shall love whenever I can.
- I will make sure that I tell and demonstrate to others that I love them.

THE MORE LOVE YOU CAN OFFER, THE MORE LOVE YOU SHALL RECEIVE.

Psychologist Susan Jeffers, whom we have already mentioned, offers a practical way to remember the principle of loving and being able to be loved. It requires maintaining a diary, which should be updated and consulted every day.

Each and every page of this diary should be headed by some positive affirmation. For example:

- I have the power, I can love and I do not have anything to fear.
- I behave with responsibility and love myself and others.
- Love is my life, and I love in all aspects of my life.

- I feel the power and love radiated by my spirit.

Under the above variable affirmations, all the pages offer an invariable affirmation. The following is what Jeffers proposes: "I commit hundred percent to every aspect of my life. I know that I am important and I behave with responsibility". And a little farther there appears another invariable affirmation: "My life is rich".

Let us now have a look at the diary book that offers a series of items that you must add on to your daily commitment and reminders. The following is the list of these daily items:

- *Spiritual growth:* in this section you should note visualization tasks and/or the objective you propose to fulfil within the day.
- *Love:* what do you intend to do to enrich your love relations: it could be a dinner invitation to your spouse, buying an anniversary gift or simply getting his or her new suit from the dry cleaner.
- *Family:* you can resolve to do things like sending flowers to your mother, call the aunt whose birthday it is, or write an email to a cousin whom you have not talked to for a while.
- *Friends:* think of a book for one of them, call another one for lunch, make a vow to fix a weekly or monthly meeting, call a friend who needs help and offer them your support.
- *Personal growth:* register yourself in a yoga course, revise your language lessons, read this book recommended to you, be regular at the gym, if you need to, start dieting.
- *Time with yourself:* read something that interests you, listen to music, take a relaxing bath, enjoy good memories, think positive, prepare yourself a cocktail, lie down and relax without thinking about anything.
- *Contribution to the community:* collaborate with an NGO or a charitable institution, participate in community meetings, collect the clothes you want to donate to the third world, donate blood, etc.

- **Work:** like other parts of your agenda, here you should commit yourself to your work-related obligations; try adding a positive touch, like congratulating some one who has had success in some project or take something to share with colleagues during tea-time.
- **Risk of the day:** underline a decision or activity that implies some risk, which you are ready to undertake; note down possible precautionary measures to make sure that it turns out well; also write down remedial measures if it turns out otherwise.
- **Today I must be grateful for...:** for my good health, for the affection that I receive, for not having any problems, for this beautiful day, for this person that I love...

At the bottom of each page, the author marks 18 points in horizontal position. At the extreme left, the word "pain" is written and on the extreme right "power". In Susan Jeffers philosophy "pain" means negative thoughts and a self-destructive attitude; "power" on the contrary is the capacity that we have achieved to control our life and destiny, the positive mental energy that energizes us to achieve, maintain and enrich our love relations and all other important aspects of our existence.

Thus it is all about placing yourself on the extreme left position or considering it as the starting point by marking it with an X. As you feel that you are progressing in your love life, getting your self away from "pain" and acquiring more "power" you can keep moving towards the right hand side of the horizontal scale. You are the one to decide the criteria of these advances, without any kind of pressure or self-deception.

Note: you may not find a proper diary to note down these elements in any book shop, but you yourself can design one such paper and make copies by printing or photocopying them as you keep needing them; you will find a model designed by Susan Jeffers herself, which appears in her book "Feel the Fear and Do it Anyway".

Affirmation of day one

I am powerful and can love and I do not have anything to fear...

I commit a hundred percent to each area of my life. I know that I am important and I behave with responsibility.

I HAVE A RICH LIFE

Spiritual growth
....
Love
....
Friends
....
Personal growth
....
Time with myself
....
Contribution to the community
....
Leisure
....
Work
....
Others
....
Risk of the day
....
Today I am grateful for
....
Where do I stand in the Pain to Power table?

• • • • • • • • • • • • • • • • • • • •
Pain   Power

The fact that this book does not offer miraculous recipes to make those we love to love us might deceive some of the readers. In fact, if this magic filter existed, its power would be completely false because it would not let you be loved as a human being and the other individual would put on an appearance of love, against his or her true desire. Fortunately, no enchantments or sorcery exist that can work against the nature of true sentiments.

If you want some one to be attracted to you or love you for what you are, you are not left with any option other than to look attractive. This does not necessarily have to do anything with your physical appearance (although you must take good care of it, especially if you are looking for love) but with your personality, virtues and sentiments. You should continuously enrich these. If you demonstrate all this, appropriately expressing your love, he or she will learn to appreciate it. If they do not appreciate it, do not waste any more time. You are following the wrong person.

Only the one who loves himself healthily, cultivates his mind and spirit and takes care of his psychic and physical health as it should be, is in a condition to love and to be loved - at least, with deep and intense love, which is the most perfect sentiment that we can aspire for in our life.

You would not be able to achieve any thing unless you cure the relation that you have with yourself. **Roma Bettoni**

Doctor Bettoni has vast experience in treating our negative aspects through positive energies and emotional intelligence. In one of her books she underlines the importance of self-esteem in emotional relations in the following words:

Love for one's self implies acting with responsibility and integrity. It means taking care of your body, mind and spirit, emotions and sentiments. To love one self means that your thoughts, actions and speech are consistent with each other. It means to try to "be" before trying to "have"; to work for personal growth, without any sentiments that limit you; to live pardoning (others) and being pardoned; to feel neither fear nor guilt: it means to live fully.

❀

All of us can agree with this image of fullness, though we may sometimes think that it might be impossible to achieve. We know our defects, our limitations and we think that we will never be able to overcome them. How can we feel love for our imperfect self? Can we develop self-esteem in spite of these negative aspects? Roma Bettoni gives us the answer:

To love is to accept, but without the need to approve. A person can be accepted as s/he is, as long as s/he is analytical with her/himself and is ready to correct what s/he does not like in her/himself or s/he thinks that is not good. I think that someone emotionally healthy tries to correct what can be corrected and accept what cannot be changed. But let's be more precise: what s/he must accept unconditionally is what cannot be changed at will (her/his place in the family, place of birth, height, colour of skin, etc.), in every thing else, s/he must accept the responsibility to grow and modify whatever needs to be modified.

It is essential for everyone first to accept and then to modify. For example, looking for a higher spirituality, to grow culturally, to control negative or violent emotions, to pardon, to live without resentment, to obtain sufficient material well-being, to analyze one's self, to criticize one's self if necessary, not just accepting errors alone but correcting these, to change in order to advance towards what is better for us and our environment.

What are the concrete tools to achieve this change? According to Dr. Bettoni, the first thing is to analyze if you are lacking in love for yourself based upon the following criteria:

- Food-related disorders: obesity, anorexia and bulimia.
- Relationship problems: difficulty in committing yourself to someone, getting intimate and communicating.
- Physical disorders: chronic diseases.
- Drug abuse, alcohol and tobacco.

- Addiction to work, frenetic activity and excessive physical exercise.
- Compulsive shopper, addiction to games of luck, sex or love.
- Dependence upon others: spouses, family, friends.

If you find yourself to be suffering from one or more of these disorders, it is very possible that you might have to fight against them in order to be able to love, and, above all, to be loved. This requires that you determine certain objectives for yourself and use your willpower and mental energies to achieve them.

Roma Bettoni thinks that for achieving personal objectives, one has to comply with the following:

- *To be simple.* The most complex tasks can be divided into smaller and simpler ones. For example, the objective of finding the love of one's life can be substituted by "I will go out more frequently in order to meet more people".
- *To be specific.* The general objective that "I will be more loving" can be substituted by a more concrete one: "I shall invite friends to my house once a month".
- *To start with a concrete action.* Instead of "I shall accept more invitations" tell yourself "when someone invites me to dance the next Saturday, I will accept with a lot of enthusiasm".
- *To reflect our values, priorities and desires.*
- *To express them in a more positive and emphatic way.*

A very fundamental element of our love life is what we call romantic love or deep love, which does not necessarily have to be platonic but intense and complete. It is this attraction we feel for someone in particular that makes us choose him or her as our spouse with the desire for a long-term relationship and the possibility of starting a family. With respect to this kind of love, each one of us, including you, might have to face one of the following circumstances:
1. You are a happy couple and you want it to last all your life.
2. You have got into a relationship recently and want to consolidate it.

3. You have just come out of a relationship and are looking for some one to love and be loved.
4. You have an unsatisfactory relationship and want a change.
5. You still have not found the right person with whom to be.

Situation number one is healthy and conventional; situations number two and three are positive attitudes with different levels of difficulty; and situations four and five need a lot of effort from you along with a little bit of luck. Thus it basically means to preserve, improve and find the relation that gives you the emotional peace and happiness that you are looking for.

If you think that you have improved as a person and continue to do so, it is time to focus on achieving your objectives of romantic love. Whatever your present state, you must put in effort to achieve what you want. The tools available to you are already mentioned in this book - use your emotions with intelligence to change your behaviour and attitude; and do not forget to visualize the fulfillment or completion of these desires.

YOU CAN WORK SUCCESSFULLY TO ACHIEVE OR CONSOLIDATE THE LOVE OF YOUR LIFE.

Achieve your professional goals

Nearly all of us spend most of our time working, studying or both. For such an investment of time and effort, it is reasonable to receive some compensation in the form of certain objectives that we want to achieve. The final aim is professional success; but it must be recognized and admired in order to be fully accomplished. No one can acquire peace and happiness if this important facet of his or her life remains unfulfilled.

You might be a student, professional, entrepreneur, artist, executive, employed, freelancer or working in any other field, the objective of achieving success will be the same. If you are lucky enough to live off the bank interest on your savings deposits or you are already retired, you might be having a hobby, which you would want to pursue with excellence. To do things correctly and be recognized for them is a positive objective and is a must for a satisfactory life. It is what psychologists call "being accomplished".

SUCCESS IS AN IMPORTANT FACTOR FOR A COMPLETE AND HAPPY LIFE.

There is a form of visualization that can be a great help in attaining your professional goals. This visualization is about working on your imagination and creativity, inventing new forms of focusing on your work and creating original solutions to the problems that might arise. This is "creative visualization" that liberates and puts at your service the most extraordinary mental energies that you can imagine. This is the kind of visualization that helps a businessman to design his shop in a very original way, a publicist to create an advertisement that makes a huge impact, an executive to propose a totally unexpected and efficient solution to a problem or an artist to find a surprising style that would make him globally famous.

Using creative visualization correctly and consciously is the key that will open the door to success.

Remez Sasson

Remez Sasson, specialist in positive thought and mental energies, has worked in the field of creative visualization. He underlines the importance of this kind of visualization in his books, courses and conferences. According to him, this kind of visualization is the key to success in all types of tasks and activities:

Creative visualization or in other words, the conscious desire and the visualization of an object, can change your life and bring you out of the vicious circle of depending only upon luck and coincidence for success. Visualizing the positive result of an effort or an idea or an action and concentrating your mental energies upon it, will lead you to success in achieving your desire. And, this is not magic. Creative visualization is a natural talent, in fact, a very powerful natural tool, a key to success.

We all, to some extent, possess and even use this talent, but negatively and unconsciously. Many of us do not control our thoughts and most of us have a tendency to think negatively. This is the reason we get negative results from our efforts. Only when you become conscious of this great mental force, analyze and learn to use it efficiently, will you see positive results.

Sasson contends that creative visualization permits us to attain very ambitious goals, and recommends its use in daily life:

I have verified that creative visualization helps us in our daily life by making everything flow smoothly and with lesser use of energy. Creative visualization continuously anticipates how things are likely to turn out in our every day life. Sometimes, what we believe pleases us and sometimes, it does not. Conscious attention to our thoughts and images can bring about a notable difference.

While creative visualization is some thing we use every day, irrespective of whether or not we are conscious of it, what Sasson is pointing out here is that we should recognize and control our visualization to achieve the success and recognition we are looking for rather than leave it to chance.

Well-being, success, money, promotion and the good things of life can be obtained through creative visualization. This does not mean that this can happen overnight. A mental attitude, perhaps a change in your attitude towards life, is necessary for this to happen. You need an open mind, concentration, the ability to visualize and a lot of enthusiasm and perseverance.

USING CREATIVE VISUALIZATION, YOU CAN ACHIEVE YOUR MOST AMBITIOUS GOALS.

The American therapist, Alison Greiner, thinks that the right side of the brain should be used for creative mental work. This should be done in combination with the other two zones of the brain, each one according to its function, providing the subconscious mind adequate images:

The language of the right side of the brain and that of the subconscious mind is the imagination. By imagining and visualizing your objectives, you will direct your secret energies directly towards fulfilling them. The ideal state of visualization means to create an effective synergy between the capacity to play with the fantasy of the right side of the brain along with the emotional energy of the central part of the brain and the rational and pragmatic focus of the left side of the brain.

The brain does not understand the difference between reality and fantasy. What you think you are, you will be. When you visualize some thing concretely and in a well-defined way, your brain starts working relentlessly to achieve what you have visualized.

The ideal visualization uses the three different areas of our brain.
Alison Greiner

Greiner says that **well known** sportspersons like Michael Jordan or Jack Nicklaus have **used** creative visualization to improve their performance; so have scientists like Albert Einstein or visionary strategists like Napoleon Bonaparte. Greiner argues that any of us can fulfil our greatest ambitions by practising visualization in a correct manner and keeping **faith** and conviction in the fact that we will achieve what we **want to**.

Similarly, she supports the contention that all three parts of the brain are used to practise visualization; Alison Greiner also recommends the practice of various kinds of visualization. Her advice includes six techniques developed by her master, Dr. Lee Pulos, one of the most recognized experts in the field of utilizing positive mental energies.

The six techniques of creative visualization by Dr. Lee Pulos

1. *Collage of images*
Visualize a collage of different images where you see yourself reaching your goal. If, for example, you aim to graduate from the university, imagine the graduation ceremony, the authorities handing you the diploma, the professors congratulating you... Unfold the diploma and visualize your name and the title on it. You must maintain each image for a few seconds and pass on to the next one within half a minute.

2. *Random visualization*
Imagine your final goal and make it appear and disappear mentally. Visualize it appearing slowly, then faster, alternating the speed, till the image is firmly fixed in your mind.

3. *Computerized visualization*
Imagine a blank computer screen, with a small dot in the middle. Place your mental cursor on this dot and make thousands of coloured dots exploding and forming the image of your objective having already been achieved.

4. Multi-focal visualization

Visualize a strong ray of light coming out of your forehead and reaching some two metres in front, illuminating your objective. New rays come out of your heart and your solar plexus and form the same image. Mentally manipulate the rays to combine them to form a three dimensional picture of your objective in front of your eyes.

5. Lightning type visualization

Imagine the current state of your objective and then visualize lightning, which makes the already achieved objective appear. This is a brilliant image and you feel full of vitality and enthusiasm. Going back to the objective of graduating from the university, in the first image you can see yourself taking a difficult exam, and then suddenly a flash makes you see yourself accepting the diploma.

6. Internal/external visualization

Imagine yourself thinking about your objective. Visualize yourself coming out of your body and reaching the objective. Again enter and come out of your body, change yourself from being a mere spectator to a protagonist. Practise this exercise several times so that your subconscious mind determines various possible perspectives that can be programmed.

> *You should be able to achieve all that you want to be, to do, or to have, with creative visualization.*
>
> **Lee Pulos**

You might perhaps think that creative visualization is not your cup of tea. That you are not ready to enter the world of imagination and fantasy given that so many concrete tasks await you and that you are currently weighed down by so many real-life problems. It is even possible that you might consider creative visualization to be counter productive; a useless distraction, a childish act that a rational adult should not indulge in. But it is precisely in the fantasy of creative visualization that you will be able to find new, efficient and surprising solutions to the problems that you find so overwhelming today.

Blocking the fantasy

Once, in one of my radio programmes, I read the six visualization techniques elaborated by Dr. Pulos. A minute later, an angry listener called and introduced himself as the director of an industrial firm. These were, more or less, his words: " I sometimes listen to your programme and it seems interesting. It has helped me learn to breathe in a better way and relax when I am stressed. But please! Do not repeat nonsense like this one by doctor Pulos! I am a mature man and cannot see myself emitting rays of light or slipping out of my body". I am sure that this gentleman was resisting a fantasy quite frequent among some people, very respectable, but totally unable to imagine any change happening in their life.

YOU MUST NOT LET YOUR PREJUDICES BLOCK YOUR ABILITY TO VISUALIZE.

The resistance to the use of visualization, or going ahead to more complex visualization processes is in fact a reflection of our ignorance of the true possibilities of our mind. It is common to assign to our mind only a rational and intellectual ability, whether big or small, and to accept it throughout our life. But we have seen that our mind, and concretely our brain, has an area exclusively dedicated to imagination, fantasy, creativity and invention, which we hardly ever use. Consequently, we do not make the best of these great dormant energies that can be activated through creative visualization.

Ursula Markham knows this topic very well and is one of the experts who has worked more than any one else on the study and use of visualization to develop the creative aspects that lead us to a true realization of our personal self. We reproduce her opinion in the following lines:

> *A majority of people possess a lot more potential than they actually are ever able to develop. This is so perhaps because they doubt their own capacity, they feel that success is "for others" or perhaps they lack so much in confidence that they can never take the first step. Only visualization can be of some help in such cases. Through visualization, we can improve our ability to learn, enhance our creativity, become more positive and perform better in certain situations, be it taking an exam or excelling in sports.*

Markham knows the different factors that can make the access to creative visualization difficult. To overcome these, she proposes an imagination exercise, which is the "first step" that we might attempt and help us move on to successive ones till we attain mastery over visualization techniques.

> *If you want to improve your creative development, we suggest a visualization exercise, which will help you achieve this. It is a type of meditation easily accessible to all, and should be used when you are searching for inspiration, be it for painting, writing or indulging in any creative activity. You will not necessarily become a genius, nor will you be able to substitute the basic technique and skills of the*

activity. But I can assure you that undertaking it will help you to extract maximum satisfaction from whatever you do and also that you will achieve better results than before.

The visualization of a walk through the garden (Ursula Markham)

I am calm and relaxed. I am happy because I know that I am working hard to improve my creative powers the way I want to. Realizing this visualization and the affirmations that accompany it, I will be more inspired to paint (sculpt, write, think…). I am starting a process that will make me happy and will give me immense satisfaction as far as my creative life is concerned.

Using the powers of my imagination, I see myself in a room, facing a door that I know connects me to the outside world. I look at the door; observe how it is made, the type of handle and the lock. Now I put my hands on the handle, open the door and get out.

I am in a path that snakes through a garden till a gate that I know is there but well beyond my vision. I start walking on the path without any hurry. I stop to look to the right and the left, immersing myself in the scenery that is being born in my mind.

Finally I see the gate and I go towards it quietly, enjoying the path and the hope of my arrival. When I am near the gate

I stop to see how it is made, of what material, how it opens, and if it is installed on a wall or railings. When I reach the gate I start becoming excited. I know that I am going to learn something about the creative direction that I am going to take in the future. I place a hand on the gate, I feel its texture; now I open it, cross it, and close it behind me.

(Let your imagination fly at this point. Let yourself fly where it takes you; do not try to influence it in any way; just stick to visualizing the images that reveal themselves before your eyes.)

I am enjoying the walk, the views and the sounds that surround me. I know that I can follow this journey as long as I want to the special places of my imagination. As soon as I want to return to reality, I will simply breathe deeply two or three times and open my eyes.

Suggestions for *affirmations*:

- My imagination is without limits.
- I can transform myself into the creative person I have always wanted to be.
- The right side of my brain is developing every day.

In moments of crisis, only creativity is more important than knowledge.

Albert Einstein

Achieve long-term financial well-being

The spiritual and the material are two complementary elements in achieving an accomplished and happy existence. It is wrong to assume that there is a situation of mental and existential well-being that looks down on all material aspects of life. Lack of money and economic insecurities are mortal enemies of the psychological and physical satisfaction that we so much want to achieve. These situations lead to anxiety, anguish and depression. They engender negative thoughts that obstruct any attempt at a favourable change to perfect our personality.

The well-intentioned stories of a content man who did not possess even a shirt to put on could have been appropriate for certain epochs or places. But it does not correspond to our lifestyles in the West, where material well-being is necessary for positive development. Therefore, it is necessary and legitimate for us to try achieving economic well-being that liberates us from the barriers that obstruct the process of our achieving perfection in other aspects of life. And above all, this well-being must be secure and long lasting.

Visualization can be of great help in liberating you from economic limitations, but they cannot guarantee that you will attain a fabulous fortune or receive an incalculable inheritance. An excessive ambition for material acquisitions could be as negative as the cruellest form of misery, especially when we are looking for psychic equilibrium and spiritual peace. However visualization, along with your intelligence and willpower, can provide you with considerable abundance.

If what you want is to be successful, you must imagine yourself to be successful.

Deirdre Jones

The American expert, Deidre Jones, points out that all successful and rich individuals started his or her fortune with a dream or a vision. She maintains that many successful entrepreneurs confess to having used creative visualization and that it played an important role in their personal and material development. If you want to emulate them, Jones offers some advice:

> *You must visualize yourself in the role of the winner that you so desire to be. Play with this mental image every time you can; imagine your earnings and perks increasing to the level you want them. Visualize your business prospering and your value growing, and the positive changes that this success will bring to your life.*
>
> *Your visualization of success must be clear, you must have a very sharp vision of what you want to achieve. But keep in mind that only visualizing for success is not enough. You must also be convinced that your objectives and goals are within your reach. This is a key concept where there is no place for paralyzing doubts. After all, if you do not believe in your self then who will?*

The element of faith, the confidence in yourself, and the certain possibility that you can achieve your goals are common to all visualization techniques. Yet this becomes very decisive when it is fortune that we are looking for. These are the areas where imaginary forces can be very powerful, and where bad luck could play an important role. As Deirdre Jones says, visualizations and affirmations must go together with a solid and absolute faith in the fact that you have the ability to achieve what you want:

> *If you want your business to flourish and if you want to have time to enjoy your prosperity, you must imagine yourself in such a situation; if you want to have a lot of money, then you must see yourself going to the bank and verifying if the balance in your account is as you want it to be. And this process of visualization must be continuous.*

Repeating your objectives aloud can be of great help. If you tell yourself about them for some time, you will start believing that this could be true. In this way, you can also fortify the faith of achieving what you want and keep your mind constantly updated about your goals.

❊

FAITH IN YOURSELF IS THE KEY TO THE EFFECTIVE VISUALIZATION OF RICHNESS.

We must keep in mind that richness or material abundance by itself is not sufficient to become a successful and happy individual. Prosperity means economic growth, but it also implies being rich in aspects like health, friendship, love, creativity and personal independence. For example, we must maintain good health and sufficient energy to be able to enjoy wealth and to be able to administer and increase it. Love and friendship give us the opportunity to share and to be generous to those we love; and independence allows us to enjoy our economic resources the way we want to, without any interference and limitation. We could say that material wealth is the objective that fulfils and optimizes other objectives that we have tried to achieve before. There is nothing wrong in it, nor in the fact that we consider material wealth an important goal of our life.

Roma Bettoni, whose work has already been mentioned in the section on self-esteem, says, "When the consciousness of prosperity is achieved, the individual is able to manifest wealth, health, well-being and happiness at any moment of his or her life because consciousness generates fortune in the Universe". And she proposes three steps to achieve this positive consciousness.

- *First step: to know how to give.* Give to others love, empathy and solidarity and whatever you can give and, if possible, a little more.
- *Second step: to be at peace with money.* If you think that money is some thing dirty or impure, your mind will keep on obeying your sentiments that favour poverty, and will isolate you from what you consider indecorous.

- ***Third step: to know that we all must win.*** It is not necessary for any one to lose for the other to win. The world has sufficient for all, without any need to plunder from each other. Get rid of avarice; everything will be granted when the time comes and as it should be.

If you have understood the message and accepted these three steps, you have a positive consciousness of prosperity. You can look for it fearlessly, because you will neither harm any one nor will you humble yourself. In order to achieve the well-being that you deserve, Bettoni has outlined ten steps of attitudes and positive actions that can work for you as a guide:

10 steps to achieve prosperity (Roma Bettoni)

- ***Commit yourself to the desires of your heart.*** The first thing is to establish contact with our deepest desires. Frequently these deep desires do not have any relation with our ideas of what we desire. On eliminating the "I should", we become like a magnet that attracts towards us the necessary circumstances needed to convert what we are looking for into reality.
- ***Decide on your priorities.*** After getting in touch with the desires that really move you, it is important to draft a plan of action that will help you to achieve them. In some cases, the priority to be accorded to each action is obvious but in other cases, you may have to organize them.
- ***Achieve a vision of your goal.*** Visualization is a powerful tool to make your dreams come true. Develop the power of your imagination.

- ***Love the options you chose.*** If you do what you love, the energies of the Universe will always support and accompany you. If you cannot do what you love, at least love what you do.
- ***Be grateful.*** Bring to consciousness the fact that all that you desire is already yours, although it is not yet manifested. It is essential to show gratitude before receiving, because a grateful heart is a heart open to receive.
- ***Accept what is offered to you.*** Being ready to accept what life has in store for you is a fundamental step towards greater wealth.
- ***Declare it like a fact.*** Once you have committed and expressed your gratitude, fortify it with words. Say for example "I take it for granted"; the spoken word has an enormous power when said from the bottom of the heart.
- ***Act.*** As soon as you start acting and see progress, you will feel a relief which will help you relax and open up to new ideas.
- ***Surrender yourself to the "true being".*** Now that you have charged up your intention with energy, thanks to visualization, you have instilled love in it, have experienced gratitude and have taken some action, the only thing to do is leave it in God's hands.
- ***Do not attach yourself to the results.*** When the farmer ploughs the land and sows seeds, he does not move the earth to see if the seeds germinate; he lets nature do her work. You must allow life and God to act freely, given that they have solutions that your limited mind cannot even think about. And even if you do not obtain the desired results, realize that there is a reason behind it. Whatever happens must always be the best for you.

5.

Spiritual and philosophical sources

Although there are many paths for searching, the search itself is always the same.
Rumi

The quote at the beginning of the chapter is by Jalal-ud-Din Muhammad Rumi, a twentieth century Sufi philosopher and poet. He is also known as the initiator of the so called "dervish whirlings". A mystic with an open and generous mind, Rumi was an exceptional guide for personal and spiritual growth with extraordinary persuasive power. His writings do not exclude anyone, nor do they deny any religious creed or thought. His ideas are addressed as much towards the Sufis as towards the Moslems, the Buddhists, the Jews, the Christians or even the Atheists. He proposes that to reach the highest state of existence, the elevated and complete perfection, is within anyone's reach. This is how he expresses it in one of his poems:

Come! Come whoever you are; Come!
The unfaithful, the religious, the atheist, it does not matter;
Ours is not a caravan of despair!
Ours is a caravan of hope!
You may have broken your vows a thousand times!
Come! in spite of all; Come!

Let's use this universal message to begin the last chapter of this book which is dedicated to a number of spiritual, philosophical and religious sources on positive thought and the use of the mental and cosmic energies through the Law of Attraction.

Hinduism: the oldest religion

The faithful man who is able to control his senses attains the knowledge that takes him to supreme peace.

Bhagavad-Gita

Hinduism was born in an indeterminate moment between the second and the first millennium before Christ. It is the oldest religion practised today and is one of profound complexity. Hinduism does not have any particular founder, either historical or mythological. In fact, it has grown with time, from a vast group of beliefs, traditions and local cults of the Indian sub-continent.

The synergetic fusion that gave rise to Hindu religion took place during the golden age of the Vedic civilization in the northern plains of India between the Indus and the Ganges rivers, with the first religious writings in Sanskrit. Amongst these, the oldest, most profound and authoritative are the Vedas and the Upanishads, followed by the *Puranas*, the *Mahabharatha* and the *Ramayana*. These sacred books deal with theology, mythology and philosophy that offer a spiritual guide to the path of "dharma" or correct religious life. The *Bhagavad-Gita* is a later text, extracted from the *Mahabharata* and is considered a complete resume of Vedic teachings.

Vedic religious teachings spread to different parts of the world through millennia. Apart from its spiritual hegemony in India, it still prevails in several parts of the world. It is calculated that today Hinduism has some 2,000 million believers of whom 900 million belong to India and Nepal. The rest is distributed among countries with populations of Indian origin like Bangladesh, Sri Lanka, Pakistan, Indonesia, Malaysia, Surinam, Guyana, Mauritius, Fiji and Trinidad and Tobago.

Hinduism has an important presence in the Western world too, especially in the diverse forms of Yoga as a technique of exercising the body and the mind and in the form of transcendental meditation. The knowledge and dissemination of Vedic belief in Europe and

America started during the British colonial rule in India. It attained a larger dimension with the extraordinary figure of Mahatma Gandhi and his philosophy of passive resistance, and also with the narrative and poetic works of Rabindranath Tagore from Bengal. After them, there were several Gurus (spiritual guides) and *swamis* (masters) whose teachings acquired considerable acceptance especially in the United States, Canada, United Kingdom and other Anglophone states.

The Beatles and the Maharishi

The idols of Rock-and-Roll, the Beatles, were responsible for the boom of Hinduism among the rebel and peace-loving youth of the Sixties in the twentieth century. This generation was also known as the generation of Hippies. In the summer of 1967, at the height of their success, the four members of the Beatles and other famous rock stars, like Mick Jagger and Brian Jones of the Rolling Stones visited Maharishi Mahesh Yogi when he was staying in England. This Hindu guru used to preach in the West "a movement of spiritual regeneration" that alarmed Christian fundamentalists. A little later, the Beatles travelled to India along with artists like Mia Farrow, Donovan and Mike Love, in order to undertake a transcendental meditation course with the Maharishi.

It is well known that Rock stars had a very intimate relation with the Maharishi, but it did not last very long.

However, it was enough for other religious establishments to accuse them of being agents of evil and also enough to term the tragic assassination of John Lennon in December 1980 as "divine punishment".

Gods in the mind

All the *dharmic* beliefs of India, like Hinduism, Jainism, Buddhism and Sikhism believe in the immortality of the soul, that is, the soul following a continuous cycle of deaths and rebirths. The ancient Vedic religion evolved towards the Hindu doctrine of Yoga, manifested in the teachings of the Vedanta. Its cosmology conceives One Universe with an omnipresent and transcendent god who unfolds himself in the figures of Ishwar (Ishwar simply means God – there is no god by the name of Ishwar in Hinduism) and Brahma.

The interesting part for the purpose of this book is that in Hinduism, human virtues are projected as smaller gods. In this belief lies the most ancient seed of the idea that God is within us. Or, in other words, every human being has a divine component in him or her. The Hindus attain this divinity through *nirvana*, a state of absolute bliss, which is attained through meditation and enlightenment.

Nirvana is neither a celestial place nor a state of the spirit, but the experience of being liberated from the barriers that prevent an individual from communicating with the divine. This includes circumstances like birth, desire, necessity, conscience, avarice, hate, ignorance, confusion and death. Each person carries a particular karma in his soul, which is the result of the good and the bad actions in his or her successive reincarnations, which, in turn, conditions the next reincarnation.

According to the laws of karma, the only way to liberate oneself from the cycle of death and rebirth is known in Sanskrit, as *moksha* (liberation) or *mukti* (redemption). It is a transcendental phenomenon that nullifies the concept of time and space and redeems the negative load of karma. This process, which leads to the state of nirvana, is not redemption in the Christian sense, but the nullification of ego, the dissolution of the individual personality. Its zenith means ridding oneself of all worldly desires and expectations in order to enter a superior dimension of serenity and wisdom.

Influence on the precursors

Undoubtedly, Hinduism, along with its philosophical variant, Buddhism, had a great impact over the Western spirituality that emerged in the final decades of the nineteenth century. The intellectuals and religious leaders, who founded and spread principles like New Thought and the Law of Attraction of mental vibrations, knew and studied Indian religions.

Although they did not share the god of mystic relinquishment recommended by these beliefs, they certainly agreed with the ideas of the participation of the human mind in an omnipresent divinity, and the possibility of being able to identify with it. They also accepted the need to overcome negativities, like depression, suffering, hate, envy, etc., to be able to reach spiritual and material goals and direct life in a positive direction.

Buddhism: The cult without God

What we are is the result of our thoughts;
It is based in our thoughts
and is made of our thoughts.
Buddha

Buddhism emerged after Hinduism and is intimately related to it. Its founder and main figure is the prince Siddhartha Gautama, a fifth century noble, who at the age of 35 attained enlightenment. Following this, he was given the title of the "Buddha" (*Buddha* in Sanskrit means

awake, vigilant and enlightened). Siddhartha preached for more than forty years, till he died at the age of eighty without leaving a single written text. His teachings rapidly disseminated throughout India and in neighbouring regions like Nepal, Bangladesh, Ceylon, (currently Sri Lanka) and China.

More than a religion of mystical content, Buddhism is a philosophical religion, a code of conduct, a path to attain perfection and spiritual serenity. Its doctrines established the "four noble truths" that address human suffering: its nature, its causes, and the way to overcome it. The fourth truth is the path to eradicate feelings of suffering and pain. This path of eight steps (or octuplo) leads the individual to spiritual serenity, to the attainment of transcendental meditation (you can attain wisdom but you can't attain meditation – meditation is something you do) and wisdom. The individual who travels this path in its entirety can be called "Buddha" because the prince Siddhartha is "the" Buddha, but not the "only" one, as there were other unknown buddhas before him and there may be more in the future.

Although some sects worship Buddha as a deity, most Buddhists venerate him only as the founder and guide who was enlightened by Universal energy, something, which did not have any beginning and will have no end. Buddhism rejects the idea of a God who is the creator, omniscient and omnipotent. This widespread atheism is the principal trait which distinguishes it from other religions of the world.

The early followers of Buddha in the West were mainly those of Asian origin like immigrants, or agnostics and atheists with some kind of spiritual restlessness. With the exception of its Japanese variant, Zen, Buddhism did not have a notable presence in the Western developed countries. But it is evident that Buddhism's rejection of suffering and its faith in the energies of the Universe inspired many mentalist doctrines in the nineteenth and twentieth centuries.

The Zen phenomenon

The World Congress of Religions, which took place in Chicago in the year 1893 was marked by the participation of the Buddhist monk

Soyen Shaku, a representative of the Zen movement. This movement appeared in Japan in the twelfth century after a Buddhist philosophical religious movement from China. The preaching of Shaku in Chicago is considered as the starting point of the meditation movement in the United States and Europe. Since then, and till today, Zen philosophy shares primacy with Yoga in terms of influence on Western practitioners of Eastern mentalism.

The special importance that Zen philosophy accords to the practice of individual meditation over the study of sacred texts, or reading of prayers and edifying aphorisms, is its distinctive trait. Wisdom must be obtained from experience, and the height of wisdom is the attainment of the "awakening" or "enlightenment" like the Buddha.

For this purpose, the disciples of Zen practise the "zazen" or seated meditation, which is the position in which Siddhartha was found when he was "awakened" or "enlightened". This posture is also in conformity with the traditional elements of mentalism and concentration included in the "noble path of eight steps".

As we said earlier, Zen is derived from the Mahayana sect of Buddhism, a sect that originated in China under the name of *chan Buddhism* in the seventh century AD. Later, chan buddhism reached Vietnam, Korea and Japan where it caught special attention. It is probable that its wide acceptance in the Western world could be, at least in part, due to its simplicity: all of us naturally have the potential to be a buddha and the only way to achieve it is by looking within ourselves. In essence, it is very similar to the philosophy of modern metaphysics and the New Thought.

Reiki: the energy that cures all

Do not attach yourself to the fantasy that nothing can be changed.
Mikao Usui

In the beginning of the twentieth century, after three weeks of fasting and meditation on the peak of the Mount Kurama, the Japanese doctor Mikao Usui conceived the ability to cure using spiritual energy. This experience drove him to develop an alternative therapy named "reiki" (from the Japanese *rei*, "universal", and *ki* "energy"), perhaps sensing that it would be disseminated to all parts of the world.

His theory assumes the presence of a "vital energy" floating in the Universe that can be accessible by trained individuals in order to use it for curative goals. The most widespread technique is similar to traditional blessing and is done by placing the hands on the affected part after both hands are rubbed to get them "charged" with therapeutic energy. It is necessary to undertake a short course directed by a "reiki master" in order to practise this method and those individuals would be able to attract reiki to their hands and use it on themselves or on others, both to cure and to prevent ailments.

The energized hands have to be placed over the patient's dressed body; the hands can also be maintained a few centimetres away from the affected zone. Some masters insist that the reiki beginner must be aware of what is wrong with the patient and concentrate to cure it, but the more radical variants do not support this principle. According to the latest, reiki itself is capable of detecting the affected zone or organs and act on them with or without the patient's will. In this way, the energies of the Universe will accomplish the three basic functions of medicine: prevention, diagnosis and cure.

In spite of its triple power, reiki can accompany other types of treatments or medication, whether allopathic, homeopathic or naturalist; in fact, this is usually done. Because this is so, some defenders of reiki attribute the cure to the universal energy while critics blame reiki when the cure does not work. However, this is not a general reaction since different therapeutic practices accept reiki, in case the patient asks for it, as a complementary therapy, or as a harmless practice.

Reiki and the New Thought

It is very probable that the widespread use of Reiki in the West is due to the simplicity of its application, the absence of mystical or esoteric doctrines and the ease with which it can be used with other therapeutic methods, the wide range of its field of action and, above all, the numerous cases of complete cure attributed to it.

Although Dr. Usui's theory is contemporary and, in some cases, newer than those of the American pioneers of the New Thought, the great popularity Reiki gained in the last decades of the twentieth century supported the mentalist philosophy, particularly in aspects related to cosmic vibrations and the Law of Attraction which are fundamental to Reiki.

Pythagoras and the Neo Platonic

Nothing perishes in the Universe; all that occurs in it is transformation.
Pythagorus of Samos

Mankind owes to Pythagoras not only the famous theorem that carries his name (in fact, he had borrowed it from the East and it was perfected by one of his disciples), but also the formulation of the first cosmologic view of scientific inspiration based upon mathematical relations that situate the Earth as one more planet of a perfect system which he called "Cosmos".

Pythagoras was born in the year 570 BC on an island called Samos, near present-day Turkey. He was trained in the thought of the first philosophers "jonios", like Tales of Mileto, Anaximandro and Anaximenes. He travelled when very young to Mesopotamia and Egypt, where he studied traditions and beliefs of the East. He fought against the tyranny of Policrates when he returned to Samos and, as a result, was forced into exile. He moved to Croton, a prosperous and cosmopolitan Greek colony in the South of Italy, and in the year 500 BC, he founded a school of philosophy, religion and politics that was famous in the ancient world.

Pythagoras taught in this school where he was adored like a God for more than forty years. Though he did not leave a single written word when he died, his disciples developed and spread his thoughts. His thoughts ranged from the field of mathematics to philosophy and the doctrine of moral asceticism. A hundred and fifty years later, his more unorthodox ideas were appraised, thanks to Plato, Aristotle and other philosophers like the "neo-platonic" philosophers of the lower Middle Ages and the Renaissance.

Pythagoreans seek to study the secret hidden in the harmony of numbers, in order to understand the harmony of the Universe. Their search was an attempt to find the essence of the Cosmos in the form of whole numbers, with a passion for numerology that drove them to intimately relate religious mysticism with science, music with cosmology and metaphysics with philosophy. The result was a harmonious synthesis of body, soul and spirit in which numbers were the "essence of all things".

The harmony of the spheres

The study of mathematics made Pythagoras fascinated with the numeric relation that exists between time and musical notes, an idea that he later applied to planetary movements. This helped him establish a perfect equilibrium between different heavenly bodies, and he named this equilibrium *music* or *harmony of the heavenly bodies* (he had already asserted that the Earth and other planets were round). This concept was clearly reflected in the books of Plato *Fedro* and *The Republic*, where he mentions that from Pythagorean cosmology, the Sun and the Moon were paradises attained by noble souls while certain planets housed hell in order to punish mean spirits.

In any case, the fundamental contribution of Pythagoras and his successors to the modern New Thought was his vision of the Cosmos as a harmonious equilibrium in constant movement, with a perfection that replaced the imperfect and discretionary powers of ancient gods. The Universe described by Pythagoras is an idealized version of what we know about it today. The metaphysicists only had to add the current scientific discoveries, like magnetic waves and transmission of energy to establish a feasible theory of the power of the mind.

Franz Mesmer and animal magnetism

There is a mutual influence among the Earth, the celestial bodies and the living beings.

Franz Mesmer

The ideas of the Austrian scientist, Dr. Franz Anton Mesmer, decisively shaped the concepts of modern metaphysicists. His conception of animal magnetism fits almost perfectly the theory and practice of the Law of Attraction; his treatments using hypnosis have been and are applied by therapists who subscribe to New Thought.

Mesmer was born in 1734 in Izang near the lake of Constanza to a forest guard. He was probably influenced greatly by Neo-platonic reading that talked of the concept of cosmic energies and, perhaps, by the life of Cagliostro and other "magicians" with amazing powers. What is certain is that he became convinced of the existence of an unknown curative force that established a relation between living beings and the earthly and cosmic energies. He named this discovery "animal magnetism", not in a zoological sense, but following the original Latin concept of *anima*, which means "soul".

Franz Mesmer was a medical practitioner and he tried to apply these concepts while treating his patients. He also tried to explain them to his colleagues. Unfortunately, the scientific society of that time rejected his fantastic theory. However, this did not prevent him from assuring his patients of his ability to channelise the mysterious forces of the universe to cure the most incurable diseases. While this increased his popularity among the general population, it provoked Vienna's Medical Association to demand that he leave the city. In the beginning, Mesmer ignored this demand, but when threatened by law, he moved to Paris to try his fortune.

In Paris, he had even more remarkable success; there was promotional support for his curative techniques when he started offering public shows in which he used hypnotism with some of the spectators. In the hypnotized state, they were made to perform impossible acts, or acts that were simply strange or funny, but never humiliating. He toured Europe as a brilliant theatrical mentalist, which made him well-known as one of the best illusionists of the eighteenth century, but not as a great scientist.

His therapeutic practices were subjected to scrutiny by a Parisian scientific committee in 1784 of which Benjamin Franklin was one of the members. The committee reached the verdict that Mesmer's theories did not have any scientific basis. This forced a resentful Mesmer to leave France and establish himself in Switzerland where he died in the year 1815. His followers continued his research and experiments despite constant opposition from medical authorities. Today, there is little doubt that mesmerism greatly influenced the development of medical hypnosis, particularly used in psychotherapy.

The theory of Emotional Intelligence

*To know others is intelligence,
to know yourself is wisdom.*
Tao Te Ching

In 1995, an exceptional thing happened: the book *Emotional Intelligence* got unprecedented popularity worldwide; it was translated into several languages and topped the list of bestsellers for a long time. This success had not occurred since the times of the interesting scientific books of Stephen Ray Gould, and gave its author, Daniel Goleman, a much-deserved celebrity status and fabulous financial gains. This was surprising given that the text of this book was immensely dense, difficult to understand and written in the style of a doctoral thesis.

Dr. Goleman, a fine psychologist with good social relations, enumerated a series of recent studies and research regarding the functioning and characteristics of human intelligence in his book. A precursor to Goleman was Edward Thorndike, also a psychologist, who introduced the concept of "social intelligence" that he defined in 1920 as the "the ability to understand and deal with men and women, boys and girls, and to act wisely in human relations".

Howard Gardner, psychologist of Harvard University published in 1983 his book *Multiple Intelligence* where he propounded the idea of the existence of various kinds of intelligences associated with different locations in the brain, instead of the well-accepted concept of a unique intelligence. He talked of eight kinds of intelligences: linguistic-verbal intelligence, logical-mathematical intelligence, corporal-kinesthetic intelligence, visual-spatial intelligence, musical intelligence, emotional intelligence (which would be divided into the intra-personal and interpersonal intelligences), naturalist intelligence and existential intelligence.

It was not Goleman who invented the expression of "emotional intelligence". In 1990, researchers Peter Salowey and John D. Mayer first defined this concept as "the capacity to perceive our own feelings and those of others, to distinguish among them, and to use this ability to guide our own thoughts and behaviour".

The feelings' thought

According to its followers, emotional intelligence consists of some concrete aptitudes within the specific abilities of social intelligence. Emotions are certainly associated with social relations, besides its role in other circumstances of our personal life. Our intelligent mind is aware of the need to establish priorities, to choose positive aspects and to reject negative thoughts that could lead us to depression and failure. The process of establishing priorities cannot be dominated by emotions, but at the same time it cannot ignore emotions completely. The goal is to identify and control emotions so that they do not interfere with our personal and social life but instead contribute information that would help us to improve our relations and decisions.

Thus emotional intelligence is characterized by four abilities:

- The ability to accurately perceive our emotions.
- The ability to use emotions to improve the efficiency of our thought and reasoning processes.
- The ability to understand our own emotions as well as those of others.
- The ability to control our emotions.

Recent research has given convincing proof that it is impossible to separate thought from emotion. The decisions that we undertake using purely logic may not be the most appropriate ones because they lack a holistic view of a situation.

The success of Goleman's book resulted in the development of two distinct groups – those who used it for training and those who used it as a theoretical premise for their work on positive thinking. The first resulted in the publication of various books that showed how to apply emotional intelligence in various fields. There were a slew of experts holding conferences and conducting courses; the author himself opted for this application in his second book named *Emotional Intelligence and Business*. There was another group of practitioners and authors involved in the self-esteem and self-help movement, who used emotional intelligence as a theoretical support for their work intending to improve willpower and suggestion power, along with a few ingredients from basic metaphysics.

No movement or author involved with the concept of emotional intelligence has ever mentioned mental energies, cosmic vibrations or the Law of Attraction. However, practitioners of the mind-related movement like Roma Bettoni, Susan Jeffers and others used emotional intelligence as a supporting component of their visualization techniques.

Appendices

Authors consulted while writing this book

- **Bettoni, Roma.** She is a lawyer who, after a process of personal search, started investigating the powers of emotional intelligence and mental energies. For many years, she was the director of a radio programme "*For all of us*". She is frequently invited to television programmes and often conducts conferences and courses. She has published *Journey to your Inner Self, Emotional Harmony* (Robinbook Editions, 2006) and *There is Another Way*.

- **Bhatnagar, Anil.** He is an expert in the field of Reiki and leads and conducts conferences on such topics as motivational therapy and personal growth. Professor Anil Bhatnagar is interested in different subjects related to spirituality and body-mind relation. His articles and books have been well received in India and other countries. His major works include the bestseller *Transform your Life with Reiki* and *The Little Book of Forgiveness*.

- **Dunwich, Gerina.** Writer and esoteric poet, she defines herself as a "witch". She has studied European esoteric practices and the *wicca* magic tradition of medieval origin in depth. In her book, *The Magic of Candles*, she describes how to use the power of candle light for concentration and meditation. She is also editor of the mystic poetry and pagan art magazine called *Golden Isis*. Gerina resides on the outskirts of Salem (Massachusetts) known for the chasing and execution of the last so-called witch in the year 1962.

- **Epstein, Gerald.** A doctor and professor of clinical psychology in Mount Sinai Medical Centre, New York, he has been treating ailments using mental images, psychoanalysis and meditation techniques for the last twenty-five years. He has delivered lectures at conferences in the United States, Europe and Israel. His works include *Waking Dream Therapy*, *Curative Visualization* and *The Seven Keys to Healing*.

- **Godefroy, Christian H.** A French mentalist, expert in mental dynamics and personal growth, he has written various books like *Passport to Liberty* and *The Positive Thought Technique* in collaboration with D.R. Steevens. His own publishing house has the maximum number of volumes in France on the subject of mental control and self-hypnosis. Currently, Godefroy lives in Switzerland and is busy with new work in this field.

AUTHORS CONSULTED WHILE WRITING THIS BOOK

- **Greiner, Alison** is a mentalist therapist, and works on positive thought and creative visualization. She has written articles for the health group *Truestar*, where she defends an optimist vision in treatment through mental therapies. Greiner has also published her articles in other specialized publications and participates in mental health programmes.

- **Jeffers, Susan** is a specialist and expert in interpersonal relations. Susan Jeffers did her doctorate in psychology from the University of Columbia, New York, and runs a private clinic in Los Angeles. With the bestseller *Feel the Fear and Do it Anyway* (Robinbook Editions, 1996) she got many prestigious awards and she became one of the best authors on self-help. Other books by Susan Jeffers are: *Life is Huge* (Robinbook Editions, 1996), *I Can Handle it* (Robinbooks Editions, 2002) and *Dare to Connect*.

- **Jones, Deirdre** is a recognized authority in the field of theoretical visualization in meteorology. She is an engineer and spends a part of her time on the research and propagation of mental visualization for personal growth and therapeutic treatments. She is interviewed frequently on television and her articles appear often in various publications.

- **Kummer, Peter** is a German psychologist, a disciple of Joseph Murphy, who spread Murphy's work in Germany. He has published many books like *I Want, I Can and I Will Get it* and *Everything is Possible* (Robinbook Editions, 1995). He has organized various courses and seminars on *Positive Thought* and participated in radio and television programmes in Germany.

- **Lewis, Dennis** is an expert in meditation and oriental therapies. Lewis studied for years the work of Gurdieff as well as Advaita Vedanta, Taoism and Chi Kung philosophies. Currently, he organizes courses for important institutions in the United States and often presents papers in conferences. He has written articles for magazines and periodicals and has published several books on good breathing and body-mind therapies. Some of them are: *Tao of Natural Breathing* and *Free your Breath, Free your Life*.

- **Mackenzie, Linda** is a Doctor in clinical hypnotherapy and author, columnist and lecturer on topics related to self-help and motivational psychology. Linda Mackenzie runs her own company, Creative Health and Spirit, and participates in radio and television programmes. She is an adviser for important public and private enterprises. Among her most successful books are: *Inner Insights - The Book of Charts* and *Help yourself Heal with Self-hypnosis*.

- **Markham, Ursula** is a recognized British therapist and hypnotherapist. Markham is an accredited member of the National Council of Hypnotherapy and is considered one of the best professionals in her field in the United Kingdom. Markham resides and works in Gloucester. She travels frequently to present papers in conferences and gives interviews on television programmes. She has published more than twenty-five books; some of which are: *The Mysteries of Visualization* and *The Answer is Within You* (Robinbook Editions, 2004).

- **Messina, James J. and Constance Messina** are a psychologist couple who specialize in the treatment of psychic and physical problems. Their technique is based upon positive thoughts and mental energies. For more than thirty years, they have been working for public and private institutions and currently they run the Coping Organization, a centre for help and orientation in Tampa (Florida). They have written various books and articles like *Advanced Development Systems*.

- **Peiffer, Vera** is a psychoanalyst and hypnotherapist. Peiffer was born in Germany and moved to the United Kingdom in 1981 where she graduated in psychology. She completed her studies with a diploma from Hypnothink Foundation and from the Hypnotherapy Centre of Bournemouth. At present, she works in London as a therapist and organizes courses on stress control in London Business School. Among her many published books the following stand out: *Positive Thoughts I and II* (Robinbook Editions, 1991-2001), *Positive Living* and *Duty trap.*

- **Pulos, Lee** is a Doctor in clinical psychology from the University of Denver. He continued his studies from the universities of Indiana and Wisconsin. Lee was a researcher and professor in the fields of mental therapies. In 1966, he received the American Association of Professional Psychologists' award on Clinical Psychology. He has been an assistant psychologist in various sports bodies and the mental trainer for the Canadian Olympic team.

- **Ragnar, Peter** is a researcher and natural therapist from the United States. He studied Taoism and practised martial arts and its influence on the body-mind relationship. Today, he is one of the most recognized masters of the art of self-help, healthy living and of longevity techniques. He is a consultant for important several government and private institutions. He delivers lectures at conferences, organizes courses and participates in radio and television programmes. He has published around twenty books, among them the bestseller *The Lifewave Phenomenon*.

- **Sasson, Remez** is an author and expert on personal growth, meditation, positive thought and creative visualization. He is editor of the bulletin "*Consciousness and Success*". Among his published books are "*Willpower and Self discipline*" and "*Visualize and Achieve*". His web page offers informative articles and practical advice on how to use mental energy and visualization to achieving success.

AUTHORS CONSULTED WHILE WRITING THIS BOOK · 179

- **Varnadoe Dow, Marty** is a prolific author and spiritual guide in the United States. She has studied oriental religion and philosophy in depth. She has a counseling website *Love can do anything*. Her books include *"Developing your Intuitive Power"* and *"Let Love Transform your Life"*.

- **Vieira, Waldo** is a medical doctor. Waldo Vieira did his post graduation in oriental philosophies in Japan. He has studied and written many books on consciousness and its spiritual projection. He is the founder of the Centre of Continuous Conscience and was the director of the International Institute of Projectology. Vieira is a member of New York's American Society for Psychical Research, and is currently supervising and coordinating an edition of the first Encyclopedia of Conscientiology.

Centres of New Thought in Spain and Latin America

• ESPAÑA

En Alicante
Aembk Alicante, Avda. Dr. Gadea 17, Entlo izda., CP 03003 Alicante; Tel: 965 253 681 / 656 388 835; email: alicante@es.bkwsu.org / www.aembk.org.

En Barcelona:
Aembk Barcelonam. Diputació 329, CP 08009 Barcelona; Tel: 932 720 843 / 934 877 667; email: info@aembk.org / www.aembk.org.
Centro de Medicina Homeopática y Biológica
Del Cós, 68, 2°, Manresa, Barcelona 08241; Tel: 938 725 777 / 938 725 960
Brusi 39, CP 08006 Barcelona; Tel: 932 008 134 / 938 722 244
Reiki Armonia
Barnnes 434, 8°, Barcelona 08022
Santa María 12, 1°A, CP 08190, San Cugat del Valles, Barcelona

En Bilbao
Centro Delta Psicología. Colón de Larreategui 26, bajo B, CP 48001 Bilbao; Tel: 944 241 960; email: ihgdelta@correo.cop.es

En Donosita / San Sebastián
Centro de Psicología Integral e Instituto de PNI Integrativa.
Secundino Esnaola 16, Entlo izda., CP 20001, Donostia-San Sebastian, Gipuzkoa; Tel: 943 291 661 / 659 808 476.

En Gijón
Centro de Orientación y Desarrollo Personal. Tel:653 539 928,, Gijón.
En Lleida
Centre Internacional New Age. Humbert Torres 16, 8°, CP 25008 Lleida; Tel/Fax: 973 244 975 / 609 949 316; email: husborrell@menta.net.
En Málaga
Centro de Yoga Integral Ganesha. Fuente Nueva 11, bajo, San Pedro de Alcántara CP 29670 Málaga; Tel: 952 787 309.
Comunidad Terapéutica Hacienda De Toros. Ctra. De Istan Km 4, CP 29600 Marbella (Málaga); Tel: 952 827 193 / 952 786 653.
En Madrid
Aembk Madrid. Orense 26, 1° pta 3, CP 28020 Madrid; Tel: 915 229 498, Fax: 915 565 764; email: infomadrid@aembk.org
Centro de Kundalini Yoga. Tel: 639 568 038; email: yoga@kundaliniyoga.cjb.net
Centro de Reiki Sambaluz. Lopez de Hoyos 120, 5° E, CP 20023 Madrid; Tel: 912 295 574 / 670 491 493; email: maestros@shambhalaluz.com
Centro de Yoga Om Ghanesa. Gran Capitán 16, Móstoles, CP 28933 Madrid; Tel: 916 475 660; www.yogamostoles.com
Centros Sivananda Vedanta. Eraso 4, bajo, Madrid; Tel: 913 615 150; email: madrid@sivananda.net
Escuela de Inteligencia de la Universidad Camilo José Cela. Jacometrezo 15 (Callao), CP 28013 Madrid; Tel: 915 488 176 / 902 151 743; email: info@escueladeinteligencia.com; www.escueladeinteligencia.com
En Santander
Centro Alisal. Los ciruelos 44, bajo, Santander; Tel: 942 339 959; email: info@centroalisal.com
En Sevilla
Aembk Sevilla. Padre Marchena 17, CP 41001 Sevilla; Tel: 954 563 550; Fax: 954 561 656; email: sevilla@es,bkwsu.org; www.aembk.org
En Vizcaya
Centro De Salud Surya. Mª Diaz De Haro 58, bajo, CP 48929 Portugalete, Vizcaya; Tel: 944 951 834; email: info@centrosurya.org

• **ARGENTINA**
En Salta
Las Rosas 140, 4400 Salta; Tel: (387) 439 5326; email: alde@arnet.com.ar
En Santa Fe
San Martín 1845, 3000 Santa Fe; Tel/Fax: (342) 459 2536; email: paillet@ciudad.com.ar
En Buenos Aires
Centro Sivananda Vedanta. Sánchez de Bustamante 2372; Tel: 4804 7813 / 4805 4270; email: buenosaires@sivananda.org

• **ARABA**
Victor Hugo Straat 5, Orangestad, Araba; Tel: 583 2110

• **CHILE**
Centro Vida Vital. La Carrera 95, Wuilpué; Tel: 926238

• **ESTADOS UNIDOS**
En Miami
P.O. Box 651600, Miami, FL 33265 – 1600; Tel/Fax: (305) 263 6712 / (305) 299 9236; email: juliestefan@aol.com

• **HONDURAS**
Pedir información al teléfono 504 232 1435

• **MEXICO**
Bosque de Inglaterra No. 18, Facc. Bosques de Aragón, Netzahualcoyod, Estado México C.P. 57170; Tel: 794 8906; Fax: 766 2591

• **PUERTO RICO**
En San Juan
Av. De Diego, Edificio Torre Museo 312, suite 503, Santurce; Tel: 724 8686

- URUGUAY

En Montevideo

Acevedo Díaz 1523, 11200 Montevideo; Tel: 598 (2) 4010929; email: montevideo@sivananda.org

- VENEZUELA

En Caracas

Ateneo de Caracas, sala B, 3er piso; Tel: 978 1753 / 978 1653

En Charallave

Calle 15, Miranda. Qta. Taguaire, planta alta, Charallave, Estado Miranda; Tel: 039 98 74 23, 938 84 05; email: zharim@cantv.net